# BUILDING A

# Relationship That Lasts

Other books by Dick Purnell

Becoming A Friend & Lover *
Becoming A Friend & Lover (Study Guide)
Free to Love Again *
The 31-Day Experiment Series
    A Personal Experiment in Faith Building
    Building a Positive Self Image
    Building a Strong Family
    Growing Closer to God
    Knowing God By His Names
    Knowing God's Heart, Sharing His Joy
    Making a Good Marriage Even Better
    Standing Strong in a Godless Culture

* Also available in Spanish

# BUILDING A

# Relationship That Lasts

# DICK PURNELL

Dick Purnell conducts seminars throughout the United States and Canada. If you would like information about bringing Dick Purnell to your city or area to present a conference for single adults, married couples or other meetings, call or write:

**Single Life Resources**
PO Box 1166
Cary, NC 27512-1166
Phone: (919) 363-8000
Web site: www.slr.org

Sixth Printing

**Library of Congress Cataloging in Publication Data**
Purnell, Dick
Building a relationship that lasts/Dick Purnell
    p.        cm.
Rev. ed. of: Beating the breakup habit. © 1984
Bibliography: p.
ISBN 0-89840-206-9 (pbk).
1. Single people—United States—Psychology. 2. Dating (Social customs) —Religious aspects—Christianity. 3. Interpersonal relations—Religious aspects—Christianity. I. Purnell, Dick. Beating the breakup habit. II. Title.
HG800.4.U6P87      1988      646.7'7-de19        87-31214
                                                                          CIP

Scripture quotations are from the New American Standard Bible, © The Lockman Foundation 1960, 1962, 1963, 1971, 1972, 1973, 1977 and are used by permission.

Published by
Single Life Resources
PO Box 1166
Cary, NC 27512-1166

Printed in the United States of America

To Paula:

My favorite date and with whom
I will never break up — until "death do us part."

# CONTENTS

BUILDING POSITIVE DATING RELATIONSHIPS
FOR SINGLE ADULTS

# ACKNOWLEDGMENTS

This is the place to give thanks to people who have helped in bringing this book into reality. I am indebted to many individuals who gave their advice and assistance. But special thanks goes to special people.

All my former girlfriends—for the experience and lessons.

Josh McDowell — for exhorting me with love to write this book.

Carol Douglass — for starting the long process of research which proved to be invaluable and for becoming my friend.

Jim Gribble — for faithfully editing many of the chapters and working on the bibliography.

Karen Holland — for tirelessly typing the manuscript.

Rocky Holland — for being my closest associate these past three years and motivating me to get the book completed.

Tina Hood — for spending many of her weekend hours typing the manuscript.

Suzanne Bourland — for keeping the office functioning while I wrote.

Janice Campbell — for transcribing all the tapes of our brainstorming sessions.

Barbara Lane — for faithfully editing many of the chapters and working on the bibliography.

Don Evatt — for taking the time to organize the research.

Paula Purnell — for constantly encouraging me to work long hours alone at my desk and giving lots of good suggestions for the book.

Dawson McAllister — for helping me to believe that I could do it.

Les Stobbe — for sticking with me even though the manuscript is one year late.

# FOREWORD

This book by Dick Purnell is way overdue.

I've known him since we were roommates at Wheaton College. I remember how impressed I was with his capability to care so deeply for people. Whether he spoke to a group or shared one-on-one, he had this rare ability to listen to the heart of a person's need, then help meet it.

So it's no surprise to me that today Dick is one of the most in-demand speakers for collegiate and young singles' groups across the country. One time, while speaking at Texas A & M, his audience grew from 250 the first night to over 1,000 the third night. I know from experience that that kind of growth doesn't happen unless the speaker effectively addresses felt needs and offers sound answers and solutions from God's Word in a relevant, practical manner.

Nearly all of us have struggled with broken relationships at one time or another. In *Building a Relationship That Lasts*, Dick gets to the heart of the matter. He looks at the reasons couples break up, and then helps us see what we each can do to build a strong, healthy relationship that will last. And the many years of counseling experience he has behind him assure us of the professional validity of his answers.

First published as *Beating the Breakup Habit*, this book proved so popular that it has now been revised, updated, and reissued as *Building a Relationship That Lasts*. The opportunity I was given to introduce this book when it first came out was one I had been waiting for for several years, and it is with great personal satisfaction that I reintroduce you to it.

A college student—after hearing Dick speak—said, "He meets us where we are. He laughs with us and he cries with us."

I know you will sense that same care, concern, help and encouragement in your life as you read this book and get to know a man who knows how to listen to your heart.

—Josh McDowell—

# THERE IS HOPE

I'll never forget her. Amy was her name. She was one of those lovely blonde Swedes with long, slender legs and a bouncy, contagious personality. Wherever she went, she seemed to be the center of attraction. As a student counselor in her dormitory at Wheaton College, she was well-liked and admired by almost everyone.

I was, on the other hand, quiet, sensitive and much less experienced in the world of dating relationships. So, I was totally enraptured by the attention she showed me.

We had met through a mutual friend and began studying together in the library. At first, we were just good friends. I'd often ask her how women felt about certain things and she'd share with me some of her frustrations and concerns about men.

Gradually, we began seeing more and more of each other. We began dating, going for long romantic walks and sharing our dreams and goals in life. As we spent more and more time together, my interest grew so that by the time I finished my junior year, I was deeply in love.

When summer break came, she went to California and I went to New Jersey. Those summer months seemed to drag into eternity. I lived and died for her letters. After my long day as a hospital orderly, I'd rush home to see if one had come. What a disappointment when the mailbox contained nothing but junk mail. But when there was a letter from her my heart raced with anticipation, and I would spend long hours writing back.

Finally, the end of the summer was near. I couldn't wait to see Amy again. I just knew my senior year in college was going to be the fulfillment of my all-American dream. At the end of my senior year, I'd have a diploma in one hand and a marriage license in the other. I was sitting on top of the world.

Then, just five days before I was to return to school, I received another letter from Amy. I went to my room, shut the door and just held it awhile. Amy's letters were always exciting to me.

I finally, tenderly opened the letter. Then the bottom seemed to fall out of my world. She began, "Dear Dick, this is the hardest letter I've ever had to write to anybody in my life." In a matter of seconds I went from ecstasy to agony. The shock of her first sentence gave me a good clue to what was coming. My heart was pounding. Tears began to well up inside. I remember the fear I felt as I continued reading, realizing that she was dropping what felt like a nuclear bomb on my head. The letter continued that she was no longer interested in continuing our relationship. She wanted to break it off. To end it just like that!

I was totally devastated. Stunned. Here it was only 5 days before my long-awaited reunion with her. My desire was to marry her. I had anxiously waited all summer to see her again. I kept thinking this must be a bad dream. A nightmare. It really isn't happening. When I see her again, everything will be okay — but it wasn't.

Back at school, I found out she also had been writing one of my friends. She had dumped me for him and within three weeks, she was wearing his class ring.

Oh, the piercing pain I felt when I saw them walking across campus, hand in hand, or studying in the library at "our" table, passing love notes back and forth.

To make things worse we had a zoology lab class together

that first semester. She sat only two seats away from me. For three solid hours, twice a week, I had to sit within a few feet of her. I wanted so much to reach out for her, but I couldn't. Every class period I was reminded again that our relationship was over. It never would be the kind of happy ending I had anticipated.

I'm sure most of you are like me. We all hope and dream about having that one special relationship. We want to love and be loved by a particular individual. After all, isn't it a let-down when the only Valentine card you get is from your mother? Or when autumn comes and the leaves start falling, isn't it a little sad to shuffle through the leaves alone? We want someone to enjoy and experience life with us. There's a whole new dimension to our world when we have that special friend to call and say, "Hi, let's go shuffle through the leaves together."

That's what we want. But that's not always the way it works in the real world. We've all experienced the trauma, pain and disappointment of rejection. Break-ups have occurred in almost everyone's dating life at one time or another, although many are not as painful as mine seemed at that time with Amy. Sometimes a couple can mutually agree to redefine their relationship in a mature, sensible manner. Yet at other times the pain is too overwhelming for some people to bear.

I read an article in *U.S. News and World Report* that started: "On June 5, a 17-year-old high school student in North Salem, New York, hanged himself with his own belt in the bathroom of his home. It was three weeks after his girlfriend, last year's school homecoming queen, took her life in a similar manner following a quarrel between the two."[1]

The article went on to say that the suicide rate for those ages 15 to 24 had risen 300 percent in the past two decades and that one of the leading causes is the pain and rejection that comes from broken relationships.

Right now you might be saying to yourself, "I realize broken relationships are painful and a part of life. I already know that because I've been there. But why? I'm tired of the same old dating pattern — on again, off again. How can I build an exciting, lasting relationship?"

A few of the many questions I've been asked as I've spoken at meetings across the country, are:

- I have dated a lot, but I lose interest after a few weeks of going with a guy. I can't seem to settle on anyone. Will I be fickle all my life?

- My boyfriend goes to school 300 miles away. Now he tells me he wants to date other girls. But I'm still in love with him. How can I keep him interested in me?

- Just before coming to hear you speak tonight, I made love with my boyfriend. We have done that several times, but I honestly don't enjoy it anymore. He should have come to hear you tonight, too. I feel guilty and used. He needs to understand what you say because our relationship is not going in the right direction. How can we turn it around?

- I've fallen in love with a woman and recently asked her to marry me. She said she needed some time to think it over. But within a month, she had broken up with me and is now engaged to another guy. I'm angry, frustrated and confused. Why did this happen?

This is just a small sampling of the many problems people have in their dating relationships. You may have had problems like these in one form or another.

I used to get very discouraged about dating. It was the same pattern every time. I would meet a terrific woman who interested me and in the beginning it would be all smiles and happiness. I'd feel she must be "The One!" Then over a period of time (days, weeks or months), disillusionment would begin to appear. Eventually she or I (or sometimes both) would say "goodbye," closing the door to any future romantic partnership. We had started with such promise and potential, but now the party was over and I would be back to square one again. Just another vanished hope or dream — just one more memory that reinforced my growing skepticism. Would I ever find a wife? Was I even capable of loving? Could I become committed to one person for the rest of my life?

As these questions cascaded through my mind, I became determined to beat the break-up habit. No matter how long it would take, I wanted to establish a lasting relationship. I wanted to have that special friend to share my life with. No, I don't have all the answers. And I cannot guarantee that reading this book will make you "disappointment free" for life. But I do have good news for you. There is hope. During my 42 years of single life I discovered many significant and helpful principles that have to do with relating to those mysterious members of the opposite sex.

We all desire to have a love that can last a lifetime. The principles in this book can help you do just that. But first, I want to help you see what I believe are the five major reasons dating relationships die. These reasons are (and we will look at one of them in each of the next five chapters):
1. Communication gap.
2. Unrealistic expectations.
3. Low self-image.
4. Selfishness.
5. Sexual burnout.

# THE PROCESS

## OF COMING

## TOGETHER

# REMOVING
# THE
# MASKS

## Breakup Reason No. 1 — Communication Gap

This was going to be a big night! Dinner, candlelight, atmosphere and romantic music. It was a beautiful spring evening in Georgia and I had picked out a fancy restaurant with great food and tuxedo-clad waiters. Paula and I had been dating for over a year. We were in love and this was my way of showing her she was the number one lady in my life.

She looked terrific, dressed in a cute white and blue outfit. When she saw me come into the room, her smile turned to a question mark.

"Is that what you are wearing tonight?"

"Sure!" I was dressed in my favorite blue blazer.

"Your tie doesn't match your shirt," Paula exclaimed.

"This is my favorite tie. I always wear this tie with this shirt."

"Well, you may always wear that tie with that shirt, but they definitely don't go together."

I was getting frustrated. I had wanted so much to look good for her on this special night but now I felt she was telling me I looked like a thrift store bargain table.

"Why don't you go put on your other tie?" she persistently asked.

"Change it? Why? I like it!" I was feeling worse by the minute. I knew that if this conversation continued long it would ruin the whole evening. I wanted to calm down. So I wrapped my arms around her, and with humor and a bit of sarcasm said, "Paula, what have I done all these years without you?"

And she quickly responded, "Well, I guess you probably made a lot of mistakes."

We both burst out laughing! It was a great icebreaker for the conversation that followed. It was clear that we had different ways of looking at clothes and styles. I preferred nice clothes with an emphasis on comfort. But Paula looked more at how colors went together. We could have had a big argument with hurt feelings to fuel the fire! But as we communicated how we felt about what was said, about our taste in clothes and about the way we tried to correct each other, we gained a deeper understanding about one another.

Fortunately, this incident did not ruin our evening. In fact, every time we think about it, we laugh. But many times, repeated incidents like this are responsible for building walls and separating people.

Good communication is one of the most critical areas in our efforts to build strong relationships.

In a study conducted by Howard J. Markman at the University of Denver, he reported ". . . the more postively premarital couples had rated their communication, the more satisfied they were with their relationships 5½ years later."[1]

And while flipping through *New Woman* magazine recently, I stopped at this statement when it caught my eye:

> The most accurate barometer of long term happiness in a relationship is how willing the two of you are to express caring and regard in ways tailored to what the other truly appreciates. *But before this can be done with any assurance of success, the two of you must get to know each other by listening to and observing what the other likes and dislikes. Then you come to understand and trust one another.*[2] (Italics ours.)

So why is it difficult to relate clearly to one another and how can we improve our communication? I'm sure we could write an entire book on all the reasons and solutions that exist, but I would like to focus on three critical areas which I feel are important for us to comprehend. They each can be a stubborn barrier to quality communication.

## Wrong Assumptions

In my opinion, one of the greatest causes of dating relationship problems is, "The Great Assumption." It can be summarized in two sentences. First, men really believe that women think like men. They don't. Second, women really believe that men think like women. They don't!

There are exceptions to every rule, but it seems men typically have compartmentalized thinking. Our little compartments are like mental mail boxes. One might be labeled girlfriend or wife; another, football; another, job; and so on. We men have the ability to flip constantly from one compartment to another so that women never know where our minds are.

For example, let's say you are in the car talking with your boyfriend who is sitting behind the wheel. You want to share something that is very personal, so you say, "I really want you to listen to this. It's something very important to me that I'd like to share from my heart."

He's sitting behind the wheel, and he says, "Uh huh, that's right, okay." But his mind is still on last night's championship basketball game.

Or let's say you're walking hand in hand with your boyfriend. Now admit it, holding hands is very important to do around friends. It plainly says to them, "Stay away; he's my territory." So you're walking along with your mind filled with good thoughts and feelings. "Oh, this is so nice and romantic. I love to hold his hand." But what's he thinking about? The muffler on his car.

A man spends most of his time in his job compartment and then next in his sports compartment. Do you know why men spend most of their time in these two compartments? It's because somehow we've been conditioned to believe that if we can gain respectability in our job or in sports, the women will love us. Unfortunately, it doesn't usually work that way.

Most of you women can relate to this. Let's say you are walking down the sidewalk and cars are cruising by. All the guys are looking for action. You come to the curb and the light is red. A car rolls up next to you, a car that looks like a shovel with the rear end sticking up in the air at a 30-degree angle. The tires are wider than the car. He's checking out the scene — you are the scene.

While you're standing there waiting for the green light, he's really wanting to impress you, so he guns his engine. As the light turns green he smokes off down the road thinking he's earned your respect. You think he's a fool.

In the book, *The Friendless American Male*, the author shares what a "real" man is like according to society's standards:

> He shall not cry.
> He shall not display weakness.
> He shall not need affection or gentleness or warmth.
> He shall comfort but not desire comforting.
> He shall be needed but not need.
> He shall touch but not be touched.
> He shall be steel, not flesh.
> He shall be inviolate in his manhood.
> He shall stand alone.[3]

With those kinds of attitudes among today's men, it's quite easy to see how wrong assumptions and poor communication can develop.

It is sad that many men have reached the top rung on their

ladder of success in business or sports, but have lost their families and relationships. We men have a great, but usually un-fulfilled, need to communicate our hearts and express who we are in significant relationships. We may get to the end of our lives with all the bucks we desire, but be left to hug only our money market funds and our lucrative investments. Personally, I would much rather develop relationships with close friends and family that are significant, loving and long-lasting.

Now on the other hand, women usually think in global terms. That means everything fits together in their lives rather than being all compartmentalized. (Many men would say that how it fits together only God and woman knows!)

Let's look at an example. You're dating this super lady and you asked her to meet you in front of the library before class the next day. But you got busy, and meeting her slipped your mind. As you're rushing off to class, late, you see her standing there and you panic. You've got to get to class, so you holler out "Hi, how are you doing? I gotta go. I'm late!" And you take off.

She stands there furiously murmuring to herself, "He didn't say 'Hi' the right way. And by the way he said 'Hi,' I know some-thing must be wrong. Where was he last night when I tried to get ahold of him? I know he's trying to tell me something and I'm going to get to the bottom of this today!"

All day long you're thinking "Man, I can't wait for our date tonight!" But while you anticipate the date she seethes and smolders. I call it "The Volcano Effect." The top will blow sooner or later.

That night you go over to her apartment for your date. You knock on the door; and when the door opens, there stands Miss Refrigerator.

"Hi, did you have a good day?" You ask.

"Yes, I most certainly did!" Cold shoulder.

"Are you feeling okay?"

"Yes, I am!" Frozen shoulder.

And then, men, we ask the world's dumbest question: "Is there something wrong?"

"Yes, Cement Brain," she thinks to herself, "there is definitely something wrong."

But she says, "No. Nothing."

"No, really, is there something wrong?" You continue prodding.

"No, let's go. We *are* going to have a good time."

Now this is when the guessing game begins. You ask, "Well, did I do this?"

"No."

"Did I do that?"

"No."

By now you are totally confused.

While all this is going on, the woman is thinking, "If he *really* loved me, he would *know* what he's done wrong."

Well I have news for you, women, he doesn't know. If you forget everything I say in this chapter, don't forget this: *You cannot assume that men will take your hints.*

You can't just assume that your date will understand. Relating takes hard work, plus lots of good, old-fashioned communication.

### Stress

In our fast-paced society, we are constantly under the pressure of deadlines and appointments. We rush to wait in line. The boss directs us to get the work done today when it will take three days. The professor schedules his final exam on the same day as two of your other finals. Your guests are coming for dinner in five minutes and you just put the baked potatoes in the oven.

Stress hits us from many angles and causes us to become anxious. In the process, we spend less quality time in interaction with our dating partners and friends.

Picture this scenario: Mark rolls out of bed around 6 A.M. After showering and shaving, he hurriedly dresses and gulps down orange juice and toast. He gets caught in the morning rush hour traffic, again. His desperate weaving in and out of traffic gives him a few close calls and a headache. His boss wants to know why the report has not been handed in yet. The traffic going home is worse than coming to work. He's late. He grabs a burger and a drink at a drive-through window and inhales it as he pulls into the driveway. He flies through the shower on his way to putting on a new shirt that he finds is wrinkled. He disgustedly looks for another one. He's late for his date which means they'll be late for the movie. After picking her up, they say a few words on the way. And when he takes her home around midnight, neither has had much opportunity to share significant personal thoughts.

This kind of schedule can work against good communication and a strong relationship, but the same scene, in a variety of ways, is repeated every day by many of us: students, single adults, husbands or wives. The pressure to produce severely cuts short our quality communication time.

When you add to that our tremendous interest in active sports, a TV or stereo in practically every room and easy transportation, it's easy to see how we can isolate ourselves and lessen our quality time with others. Real communication takes time.

**Pride**

This is the most difficult barrier to deal with because it reaches to the depths of our being. We like to run our own lives, to think no one can tell us what to do. Intimate communication takes vulnerability and honesty. If someone gets too close, we may rebel and pull away — "It's my life."

J. Grant Howard, in his book, *The Trauma of Transparency*, writes about how, since Adam and Eve, we have been wearing masks.

> Many terms are used to depict this tendency we all have to hide from one another. We cover up our needs. We bury our thoughts. We repress our feelings. We mull things over inwardly. We are quiet, reserved or even withdrawn. We are introverted. Sullen. Pouting. Shy. Bashful. We say, "I couldn't care less," but we really do. We say, "Leave me alone," because we don't want anyone to step inside and see what is really happening. We say, "I don't want to talk about it," even though we desperately need to. We say, "Nothing is bothering me," when in all honesty a problem is clawing our soul to shreds. We say, "I can work this out myself," when in reality we can't; we need help . . . Not simply because we are fearful, bashful, inarticulate and confused, but ultimately because we are sinners. Sin separates. Sin alienates. Sin causes people to hide from one another.[4]

I personally can relate to what he is saying. There are many times I have not communicated openly and honestly because I was hiding.

But when we truly experience God's love and forgiveness in our lives, we realize we no longer have to hide. We are okay as we are. And we can share our deepest thoughts and feelings with one another. We can be set free from this bondage of pride and self-centeredness which the Bible calls sin.

So what are the ways we can improve our communication and build intimate, longer-lasting relationships?

### Build trust.

You say, "Hey, what does trust have to do with communication?" Almost everything. To communicate yourself requires that you let someone see inside you. If you were a parent, you would not leave your child with someone you did not know and trust, someone you had not spent time with or had a chance to observe. The same is true of our communication.

Harry Zehner quoted a number of psychiatrists in an article he wrote for *Cosmopolitan* magazine entitled, "50 Shrinks Give Their Rx for Marital Happiness." One of them was Irwin M. Marcus, M.D., clinical professor of psychiatry at Louisiana State University Medical School. He says: "Out of trust comes honest communication and understanding. Without trust, communication and understanding, a couple cannot really get to know each other."[5]

Other people can trust you when you keep confidential something they have shared, or when they can share how they really feel about something and not be judged. Genuine trustworthiness is a wonderful quality to possess and find in a relationship and is a cornerstone from which good communication can be built.

**Learn to open up.**

C. S. Lewis has said, "To love at all is to be vulnerable."[6] We should stop letting fear determine how we communicate in our relationships.

We all want to be loved, but we can only be loved to the extent to which we allow our "real selves" to be known. If you wear a mask or put up walls to protect yourself and then someone says, "I love you," what do they really love? The extent to which you have hidden yourself from them is the extent to which their love can be questioned. You will always fear that they love only the part of you that you have let them know. We must learn to be open and vulnerable in relationships.

Maj. Britt Rosenbaum, M.D., Associate Professor of Clinical

Psychiatry, Montefiore Hospital and Medical Center, New York City, says:

> Most simply, you must dare to be yourself and show your feelings as much as possible, despite the risks involved. Relationships often get into trouble because feelings that are deemed unacceptable are closed off: "I can't tell him *that* . . . It might hurt our relationship." In fact, [when you do that] you are protecting your own feelings, and this may not be your partner's response at all.[7]

**Men, share your feelings.**

As we just mentioned, opening up is vital to the relationship. But so often men seem to shy away from open, honest communication.

I was at a critical turning point in my life a few years ago. I had decided to leave my job, but I did not know what my next step should be. Confusion filled my mind as I looked at several options. Should I get a job, go to graduate school, teach, start my speaking ministry at universities across the country or do something else? What should I do? What direction was best?

I was dating Susan during this questioning period in my life. She was a good friend and I enjoyed her company a great deal. In the course of our conversation, she asked me what I was planning to do in the future. As I began to explain my situation to her, the frustration and confusion overwhelmed me and I started to cry.

My immediate thought was, "Oh boy, if I continue to cry, I will probably lose Susan. No girl wants a crybaby for a boyfriend." But I knew that to stop crying, I'd have to suppress my real feelings and frustrations and could not be honest with her.

I had to tell someone, so I decided to share with Susan all my thoughts and emotions. For the next thirty minutes I poured out my heart and feelings.

Finally, I asked, "What do you think about all this?" I expected her to reject everything I had said, and reject me for showing weakness.

Without a moment's hesitation she said, "Seeing you be so real and vulnerable just makes me love and respect you more."

I was both shocked and pleased. But I found then that a woman wants to see a man's heart, not just hear his thoughts. I'm not advocating that men sit around and cry a lot. But I strongly believe that you need to allow the woman to see the real man inside your heart. She'll love you even more.

### Women, encourage men to share their feelings.

Men find it much easier to tell you what they think about something than how they feel about it. It can be very difficult for them to open up but your encouragement and sincere, gentle questioning can go a long way.

I have found that some women have a real ability to draw a man out of himself, providing it is not done in a pushy or insensitive manner. I think this can be a tremendous asset to a relationship. Women, be sure to ask the man how he *feels* about certain things. Listen to what he says and then be willing to share your own feelings in return.

### Plan time to talk.

Probably one of the biggest challenges in dating today is to plan conversation. Most of our activities center around little or no significant interaction. We spend much of our time together going to movies or concerts, watching TV or attending spectator events.

One of the easiest dates in the world is for a man to take the woman to a movie. Here he can pay someone else just $6.00 a person to entertain them for two hours. He hardly has to say a word!

Activities like these do not allow or encourage much opportunity for us to interact in depth about who we are, or share our goals, hopes, hurts and loves. We need to set aside time each week to just talk with each other. It can do wonders in building understanding and caring.

**Listen and show interest.**

Many books have been written on the value of listening. You all know what it is like to be sharing yourself with someone, then realize the person is not even listening. It communicates that that person is not really interested in you.

We have a tendency to think it is only our words that communicate. Yet, that is only 50% of interaction. The other part — just as vital — is listening. It can often be harder work than talking.

It not only means hearing every word, but understanding as well. One of the best ways to show genuine interest is to be sensitive to a person's feelings and to express care and empathy.

**Ask for forgiveness.**

One of the fastest ways to build walls that block communication is to hurt someone, even if unintentionally. It takes a mature person and true friend to ask for forgiveness. When things get rough, it's easy to let things slide or to ignore them. We tell ourselves, "It will take care of itself," but bad feelings may smolder and build toward something much like a violent volcanic eruption.

Is there anything you need to ask forgiveness for? Do you have a close friend you need to tear down a wall with . . . and build a bridge? It is usually not the easiest thing to do, but the reward is always worth it.

You also will find that communication comes easier when you feel clean in God's sight. Remember, sin makes us want to hide. Ask God to forgive you of those wrongs, then accept His forgiveness and know that you stand clean. Now you are better able to communicate openly with your friends and with the person you are dating.

# HANDLING
# UNREALISTIC
# EXPECTATIONS

## Breakup Reason No. 2 — Unrealistic Expectations

Seldom in life is there only *one* reason something good or bad happens. When a relationship breaks up, usually many factors come into play. However, according to psychiatrist Allen Fay, M.D., Mount Sinai Medical School, New York, "One of the biggest problems [in relationships today] is unrealistic expectations."[1] I, along with many others, agree. By unrealistic expectations, I mean that one or both of the people involved expect from their partner more than is possible. Their idea of what the relationship should be was conceived in a fantasy or dreamland rather than in the real world.

We've all heard the phrase, "Love is blind." In fact, I'm sure most of us have been blinded once or twice. We see only what we *want* to see in the other person and we believe that being with that person will make everything else in life turn up roses.

Author Norman Wright in his "Guidebook to Dating" says,

> Too many young couples [are] blinded by unrealistic expectations. They believe the relationship should be characterized by a high level of continuous romantic love. As one young adult said: "I wanted love to fulfill all my desires. I needed security, someone to take care of me, intellectual stimulation, economic security immediately — but it just wasn't like that!" People are looking for something "magical" to happen . . . But magic doesn't

work; hard work does. When there are positive results it is because of two people working together one step at a time.[2]

I had expectations of Amy making me happy. As long as I was with her it seemed I was the envy of all my friends. I believed she would fulfill all my fantasies. At times I felt unattractive, but I thought being with her would suddenly make me attractive. I would become more popular and outgoing because that's the way she was. I would become a *man* because she seemed to be such a *woman.*

There were many other factors I'm sure, that put an end to my relationship with Amy. However, in retrospect, I'm confident that if we had eventually married, it would have been a disaster.

Years later, when I was able to see Amy with both eyes open, I realized I had overlooked many things. She was extremely immature and unsettled, going through one relationship after another during her college years. The fact that she had dropped so many other guys hadn't registered with me then. Later, after seeing the direction her life took after she graduated, I saw how our lives had been going in two different directions all along. I had made her a goddess simply because this fantastic woman had shown me some attention. The problem was that she fit better into my dream world than into my real world.

I was a lovesick guy back then, no doubt. But each of us is guilty of wanting to find in someone else the fulfillment of all of our deepest desires and needs. We attempt to make the person more than reality allows, and it sets us up for disillusionment and disappointment — even bitterness.

According to Dr. Robert Sollod, Associate Professor of Psychology, Cleveland State University (quoted in a book by Jacqueline Simenauer and David Carroll),

> . . . these overblown expectations may hint at the reasons why so many singles' relationships fail. Often neither person begins dating with reasonable expectations; both may have impossible standards. When these standards aren't met, instead of realizing that no one will *ever* measure up to our ultimate ideal, both parties

break off and go in search of the unattainable.[3]

As disillusionment and rejection set in, the bubble bursts. Suddenly you have a rude awakening — your partner is not the person you thought he was but only the object of your unrealistic expectations. This person has not made you totally happy and fulfilled, and sometimes is even grouchy, unloving, insensitive and unreasonable.

So, disappointed, you do one of two things. You leave to search again for "the right one," — the person who is exactly the way you dreamed and fantasized, or you set out to remake your partner and change him to meet your desires and ideals.

Now it is true that we can all stand a bit of improvement. In fact, there will be room for change and growth during our entire lives. But one of the fastest ways to create tension and distance in a relationship is to continually try to make significant changes in your partner. The deepest desire for each of us is to be loved *for who we are,* to be accepted, faults and all. To attempt major changes in your partner is to say, "I'll love you — if . . ." And that is really not love at all.

Josef H. Weissberg, M.D., Assistant Professor of Psychiatry, Columbia University School of Medicine, New York, says:

> One common difficulty in contemporary (relationships) stems from the idealization that is so frequently a part of romantic love. When the idealized partner inevitably falls from his pedestal, the idealizer's disillusionment and anger is often extreme. My best advice would be to take a long, hard look at your partner, become familiar with his liabilities as well as his assets, and be quite sure that you can live with both, *without* changing things you don't like. Love at first sight is fine . . . *if* it is followed by realistic appraisal and acceptance.[4]

That sounds like terrific advice to me. But how do we do it? We can deal with unrealistic expectations better if we know what they are. So, what are some of them?

**"Our partners will act like our parents did."**

First, we expect our partner to behave in a manner similar

to our parents. We sometimes forget that our partner had a different set of parents and influences in life, and, more importantly, that that person is a unique creation, unlike anyone else in the world.

I learned this the hard way soon after Paula and I were married. For six weeks we traveled, speaking at conferences and meetings in several states. We finally arrived at our apartment in California, glad to be "home" and ready to begin the process of settling in. That Wednesday, Carol, a friend of Paula's came to stay with us for awhile. When I got up Sunday morning, I couldn't wait for a big breakfast before going to church. After getting ready, I waited for my meal. But though I was all ready to go — and hungry — Paula was in the bathroom fixing her hair. I looked at the clock again, getting more upset as each second ticked by. Finally she came into the kitchen. "Where is our breakfast?" I asked sternly.

"There is plenty of food in the refrigerator and cabinets for you to eat," she replied. Then, noticing my irritation, she asked, "Have you been waiting for me to fix breakfast for you? You are all ready to go and I have a lot to do. Besides, Carol and I don't plan to eat any breakfast."

Still boiling underneath but working hard to keep my cool, I persisted, "It's too late now for any eggs and toast. But how about at least getting me a grapefruit?" Now we both were definitely irritated.

"Here!" she angrily replied as she plopped a grapefruit on the plate in front of me.

"But it's not cut up!" I — a mature, newly-married man — was losing my composure in front of our first house guest. What a great way to start a Sunday. I doubt that I even heard a word during the Sunday morning worship service. I was too busy smoldering.

That afternoon, we discussed our tensions while Carol was

visiting some other friends. Why did we have such a difficult time at breakfast?

It finally hit me. In my home, Sunday breakfast was always special. Mom would get up long before us kids and fix a delicious breakfast. It was a Sunday morning family tradition to have special waffles or pancakes or eggs, unlike any other morning of the week. Mom probably did that at least in part to motivate us to get up and get ready for church. But it was also a special family time in our home.

That was a tradition in my New Jersey home many miles away from where Paula grew up in North Carolina. In her family, her dad often would fix his own breakfast, and occasionally would fix eggs for everyone.

I expected Paula to act like my mom and serve a big family style meal. She expected me to act like her dad, and simply fix my own food. After discovering our hidden expectations, we laughed. Then we developed a plan that would satisfy our unique needs and desires and solve the Sunday morning breakfast problem.

### "Our partners will meet all our needs."

Second, it is an unrealistic expectation to assume our partner will fill up the holes in our lives, especially where we feel we are personally inadequate. That was exactly what I had expected from Amy.

Philip J. Guerin, M.D., a family psychiatrist in New Rochester, New York, says, "The bottom line (in a healthy relationship) is taking responsibility for your own happiness and well-being."[5]

That's hard for us to do. It's much easier to let someone else be responsible and to expect that person to take care of us. But we can never find real happiness and fulfillment in our relationships if that's our approach. So if you find yourself looking to someone else to meet all (or most of) your needs, know that you are developing unrealistic expectations. No one person can meet all your needs. (We will take a more in-depth look at this in chapter 5.)

### "Life's problems always will be solved easily."

Third, we expect easy solutions to the difficulties we encounter. The media often reinforces this attitude. Now let me say up front that I have no intentions of tearing down the advertising or entertainment industries, but I do want you to recognize clearly that "what you see is not necessarily what you get." Real life is much more complicated than what the media tends to portray.

I think we are all aware how profound an influence TV programs, movies, and magazines have in our lives. In many ways they influence us in determining the kind of dating partners we want, and what we are supposed to be like to attract them.

Did you realize that by the time a person graduates from high school he has watched an average of 18,000 hours of TV? (That's 5,000 more hours than he has spent in school.) Nearly every program a person watches portrays problems being solved by actors who seem to have it all together. Within 30 or 60 minutes they usually both define the problem and solve it.

During those same thousands of hours of TV watching, that person has also seen approximately 200,000 commercials, each one proclaiming in 30 seconds that that product will bring you happiness.

One of my all-time favorite commercials is an old toothpaste ad. The Purnell version of this ad goes like this: Miss Stewardess goes into the cockpit to serve coffee to the pilot. The problem is, she has the world's worst disease — *yellow teeth*, without a doubt, one of the most horrible plagues in America.

She says to the pilot, "Hello there. Would you like some coffee?"

We can see easily by the pilot's expression that he is thinking, "Coffee? She has yellow teeth. No, thanks!"

So she walks away, dejected.

Isn't it amazing how in every one of those commercials there is a good friend close by who has all the right answers? The friend says (with a big glistening smile) "This is what you need. Bright-O toothpaste."

Ta da, ta da. A giant tube appears on the TV screen shooting laser beams! One even hits her right in the mouth. All of a sudden, her disease is gone! Her teeth now radiate whiteness. And we all stand to our feet and cheer.

The next day she re-enters the cockpit, asking once again, "Would you like some coffee?"

The pilot, with adoration in his eyes now, says, "Oh! White teeth! Of course, you can pour me coffee any time!"

Now the commercial was hammed up a bit as you can see, but the underlying message is the same. Isn't it ridiculous? Here was a woman who was rejected by someone she apparently wanted to please. But in a matter of seconds, she had found the solution . . . and along with it, apparent happiness and love.

But life doesn't work that way (not for anyone I know, anyway). Sometimes working through a relationship problem can take weeks or even months of understanding, patience, prayer, forgiveness and tender loving care. Sometimes there may not even *be* the kind of solution we are expecting or hoping for.

If you find yourself expecting to be able to work through every difficulty in your relationships easily and quickly, then you are not being realistic. True intimacy cannot be reached in a relationship without first resolving these problems together. This takes time, hard work, determination and commitment. But the result can be a happier, more satisfying relationship.

**"We will find a perfect partner."**

Fourth, we desire our partner to be like society's ideal. This is another area in which the media may have affected us. It may have developed in us a false standard for desirable qualities in a mate. Frederic Flach, M.D., Clinical Associate Professor of Psychiatry, Cornell University Medical College, New York, says:

> . . . the people to whom we are most exposed [through the media] have become models to be admired and emulated. As a result, the celebrity has replaced the hero on center stage, and society is in danger of losing sight of those characteristics — such as courage, sacrifice and generosity — that have been central to human survival.[6]

Much of the time, media portrays the image that happiness and personal fulfillment is gained by being beautiful, owning the hottest car, drinking the right beer, wearing the right clothes, being a superb athlete, knowing people of influence and (let's not forget) being sexy.

Every advertising expert knows that sex sells products. I was watching a TV commercial for a car the other night. The announcer was listing the benefits of the car, one of which was "a sexy dash". Now I must ask, have you seen a sexy dash lately? Have you ever gotten up in the morning and sat in your car and said, "Oh, you sexy dash"? I am a counselor, and my advice to you is, if you do that, please find professional help. You have a problem.

Many men have developed their ideals from photos of beautiful women. *Playboy*, *Penthouse* and other magazines have become very successful publications by capitalizing on that. But let me ask you men something. The last time you were gazing bug-eyed at one of those lovely ladies, did you see a pimple on her nose? You say you weren't looking at her nose? Well, if you had been, you would have found no blemishes — on her nose or anywhere else. She was perfect. And that's the problem. Nobody's perfect. If you know anything about photographers, you know they'll take hundreds of pictures before they find one good enough to use in a magazine. That perfect photo portrays the exceptional rather than the normal. It is not realistic.

In real life, beautiful women sometimes have pimples, blemishes, messed up hair, smudged mascara or spots on their dresses.

Have you ever noticed how few of the famous stars in movies are unattractive? Most of the men and women are knock-outs. The ugly people are usually the bad guys, the undesirables.

When you flip through magazines, the models in the ads are all so terrific. But the temptation is to look then at your partner and say, "Boy, what a letdown!" That's the difference between an ideal and a reality.

### "We will have a glorious romance."

Fifth, we unrealistically expect a fantasyland romance. Romance novels appeal to the fantasy side of our natures. These stories seem to be especially popular with women and are sometimes called escape novels. The writers exquisitely describe dreamy scenes in which the woman, aching with desire, is ecstatic as her strong, passionate lover sweeps her off her feet. It is so mysterious and thrilling. It's a dream world, yet they sell millions of books. Does it have any basis in reality? Are these real men? Could real dates be like this? Hardly.

Romance is a mood, a feeling that the writers want you to

experience as you watch the movies or read the magazine articles and books. But when you try to experience it in real life, it is not the same. In reality, the man is awkward, and the telephone rings while you are kissing. The feelings never seem to last long enough, and he doesn't quite understand all your needs, as a romance novel portrays.

Janet Dailey has authored 79 romance novels and is one of the world's best-selling authors. She was asked about what sort of behavior or attitude in a man is seen as romantic.

> On the whole, I think it's thoughtfulness. In courtship, a man can't do enough for a woman. He tells her she looks nice, gives her flowers, kisses her hand, is attentive to everything she does and says. Disillusionment with marriage sets in at the point when he stops acting that way, and the woman feels a tremendous loss. She has lost that wonderful part of courtship when she felt important because he treated her as if she were the most important person in the world.[7]

It is certainly true that all of us should bend over backwards to be thoughtful and considerate with each other. But what man can cater totally to a woman's every desire and need? A man has weaknesses and faults, just like a woman. Obviously these prevent him from being the perfect lover found in romance novels. So we move from person to person hoping to find that dreamlike love. It's no wonder we have so many broken relationships in the "real world."

So what are some ways to handle unrealistic expectations?

### Accept the facts.

One way is to accept the fact that we live in an imperfect world and are imperfect people. No one has it all together, not you, and not your partner. There is no such thing as the "perfect couple." We are all in the process of learning, developing and becoming. But, if there are major changes you would like to make in your partner concerning that person's relationship with God, friends, purpose and direction in life or physical features that disturb you, you probably should not be dating that person now.

Richard Rabkin, M.D., Clinical Associate Professor of Psychiatry, New York University School of Medicine, says:

> . . . you'll discover that your partner is not perfect. There are two types of imperfections: Those you can't do anything about, like his/her mother, and those you can, like his habit of leaving his shoes in the living room.[8]

Life is a schoolroom. We each learn, grow and develop with the help of friends, God and life experiences. Be patient with yourself and with the person you are dating. God isn't finished with either of you yet. You need to encourage each other to be the very best you can be.

And remember, disappointment is a part of life. God hasn't promised us a continual Disneyland. Life is not a bed of roses. There is no contract or guarantee that we will never be hurt by broken promises. In fact, disappointment can be a tremendous teacher. My experiences with Amy and others taught me valuable lessons that I have applied to my life. My life would be poorer without those tough learning and growing experiences.

Corrie Ten Boom, a single woman who lived through a World War II Nazi concentration camp, said, "God develops spiritual power in our lives through the pressures of hard places."[9] Many great people have turned their disappointments and failures into stepping stones of success.

Abraham Lincoln, for example, was defeated five times before winning an election. He suffered a bankruptcy and a mental breakdown. He was also rejected by a woman he loved. But he — as can all of us — used the failures for stepping stones to success.

**Build on mutual interests.**

Second, in overcoming unrealistic expectations, you can build on common ground. Our culture tells us to be individuals and to go for what we want. But in a relationship when two maturing people spend lots of time together, there is a tremendous need to find harmony. Be realistic about each other's strengths and weaknesses, habits, behavior patterns and attitudes. Seek companionship, not perfection.

> Marriages that succeed are based upon a realistic approach to the creating of a partnership. The partners recognize their individual imperfections, and understand that a mixture of needs and anticipated rewards motivate every action and reaction. More importantly, they choose a partner who has similar goals, compatible interests, complementary intellect, and some mutual beliefs. The most important of the mutual beliefs is certainly that marriage is a form of sharing of life's real problems and its joys. It's not an endless romantic encounter.[10]

**Learn from others.**

Third, seek helpful insights from other people about handling unrealistic expectations. Talk with a couple who has a happy and fulfilling relationship. Don't be embarrassed about asking them to share with you what they've learned from their experience.

Paula and I did this while we were engaged. Several married people counseled us and helped us file down our rough edges and spot potential conflict areas. Even at our wedding rehearsal the night before we got married, we asked the invited guests to give us their insights on what makes a good, loving marriage. We have benefited tremendously from their wisdom.

**Find permanence.**

Fourth, and most important, put your hope in something

that will last. Jesus is the same yesterday, today and forever. He is always true to His promise. He will never build you up just to let you down. He will never deceive you or paint an unrealistic picture of His love for you.

Allan Loy McGinnis, in his best-selling book, *The Romance Factor,* says:

> We are programmed by our culture, by the depiction of love on the screen and by popular songs, to think of love as the major solution to all our problems. It is the holy ground which, if recovered, will bring ultimate happiness. This is a disastrous path, for we are expecting romance to give us something that only religion is designed to offer. When we begin to worship romantic love, it collapses under the weight.[11]

Many times we are guilty of pursing our ideal romance to the point that we — in fact — are worshipping the idea or the person. But if we worship anything other than God, the creator of the universe and the author of love, we are setting ourselves up for disappointment. No one but Jesus can ever satisfy us or meet our expectations.

Keeping our spiritual life in balance is one of the best ways to guard against unrealistic expectations.

Here are some excellent questions to ask and discuss with your dating partner. Learn from each other about your expectations, hopes and dreams.

1. What are our common interests?
2. What expectations do we have of each other?
3. How do we react when these clash? What is a good way to resolve this?
4. Which of the above mentioned expectations are unrealistic, and why?
5. What steps can we take this week to work at establishing better harmony in our relationship?

We have looked at a few simple steps to counteract the difficulty of unrealistic expectations. But there is another reason relationships are damaged. I consider it to be one of the most important reasons of all. In the next chapter, we will look at how self-image can destroy a relationship.

# LIKING YOURSELF
# SO OTHERS CAN TOO

## Breakup Reason No. 3 — Low Self-Image

Josh McDowell and I were roommates in college. On weekends, Josh would go someplace to speak and then come back with glowing reports of 200 to 300 people who attended his weekend meetings. It really began to frustrate me.

One of the things I had always wanted to be was a good speaker. But while Josh was out speaking to hundreds, I would have a little Bible study with three or four friends at the most. Over a period of time, I started getting jealous of Josh. I wanted to be popular like him. And I began comparing nearly every aspect of my life with what Josh was like.

During college, neither Josh nor I ever discussed these feelings. But nearly eight years later, I learned from him that he was jealous of me, too. He felt that I was much more effective than he in discipling new Christians and in helping people come to know the Lord.

Isn't it funny? Both of us were wishing we were more like the other — because we had not fully understood and accepted our own unique, God-given qualities and characteristics.

Do you often compare yourself to others?

Are you critical of yourself or others?

Do you often put yourself down?

Do you have a difficult time expressing your feelings and thoughts?

If you answered yes to any of these questions, you may be

having trouble with your self-image, but that wouldn't be surprising. Most of us, in one way or another, battle feelings of inferiority and low self-image.

As I have traveled and spoken to hundreds of audiences and people from every type of background, the opportunity to counsel young, single adults has been a regular part of my life. But over and over, I've been amazed by the number of people who come to me who don't like to accept themselves.

Why do so many of us struggle with this? How does it cause relationships to break up? And most importantly, what can we do about it? Before we look at those answers, let's first look at several factors that contribute to a low self-image.

### Other People

Do you let others determine how you feel about yourself? Someone has said:

We are not what we think we are . . .

We are not even what others think we are . . .

We are what we think others think we are.

Most of us can relate to that. But why do we give other people that kind of power? It was never intended for others to determine how we feel about ourselves. When a person's self-concept is based on what he thinks others think, then his image of himself will always be changing. This basis of evaluation is fickle, because people's attitudes and opinions are constantly changing. If we value ourselves today based on what others say is valuable, then our self-esteem may be damaged tomorrow. Dr. James Dobson, writing in *Hide or Seek,* tells about Dr. Maxwell Maltz, the plastic surgeon who authored *Psycho-Cybernetics.* Women used to come to him requesting that their breasts be reduced in size. Today they are asking that he pump them up with silicone. In King Solomon's biblical love song, his future bride is ashamed of her dark skin that had occurred from exposure to the sun. In their day, a suntan was degrading. But now the brown bride would be the "beauty" of the beach.

Women today are ashamed to admit that they carry an extra 10 pounds of weight, yet Rembrandt, the famous Dutch painter, loved to paint plump, round bodies. Dr. Maltz continues "Don't you see that your personal worth is not really dependent on the opinions of others and the temporal, fluctuating values they represent? The sooner you can accept the transcending worth of your humanness, the sooner you can come to terms with yourself."[2]

Primarily, we let others determine our value in three areas of life: beauty, performance and status. Let's take a brief look at each.

*Beauty: How do I look?*

As we are all aware, our society places a tremendous emphasis and value on beauty. The message is subtle but it is communicated in many ways:

Advertisement: "You too can have beautiful skin."

Friend: "Don't Tom and Sue make a good-looking couple?"

Date: "Bob's girlfriend sure is gorgeous, isn't she?"

Now if you're thinking, *Other people's opinions of how I look really don't matter,* then let me ask you this question. How do you feel when someone volunteers to either compliment or criticize the way you look? Their compliments can send you flying and their criticism can cut deep. Other people's opinions definitely can determine how we feel about ourselves.

*Performance: How am I doing?*

After beauty comes intelligence and performance. If we feel our achievements approach or meet the aspirations of our friends or family, we have higher self-esteem. But if we feel we are not achieving as much as others think we should, we can really feel down on ourselves. This is communicated in some of the following ways:

Parent: "You can do better than that."

Friend: "I can't believe you're still living at home!"

Relative: "When are you going to get a real job?"

Since childhood, most of us have been encouraged to excel and get ahead. So, regardless of how well we've done, we often think we should have done better. And if we feel like we never have done quite good enough, we can easily get discouraged. It can bring on a deep sense of inadequacy.

*Status: How important am I?*

We often allow others to determine our value and worth. Have you ever heard these statements?

Employer: "We've decided to hire Tom instead. You don't have the qualifications."

Friend: "We had a party, but forgot to invite you."

Family: "Dad has a business trip so he's just not going to be able to come."

Date: "I think we should be just friends."

Almost everyone has the unspoken desire to be respected, wanted and admired. And usually, we feel bad if we are ignored, if our name is forgotten or if someone makes us feel unimportant. But our true value and importance is *never* determined by what others think. More on this later.

Those are three of the primary ways we allow others to determine our self-esteem. The second factor contributing to a low self-image involves what we do.

## Our Behavior.

When Adam and Eve sinned in the garden, guilt and fear made them want to hide. Both knew they had done wrong and were not proud of their actions.

Margaret, a friend of mine, recently shared the following with me: When she was 7 years old, she noticed that the nice, old lady living in the big house next door was preparing to move away. In the process of packing up all the belongings of her long-time home, she decided to give many things away. This included several children's games and toys. But there was something else Margaret had kept her eye on.

Some time earlier, as she was playing in the yard, she saw a beautiful, fragile vase sitting outside a basement window. Every time she passed that window, her desire for the vase grew. One day, she could resist no longer, and she took the vase and hid it so it would be hers after the old lady moved away.

But Margaret remembers that, after taking the vase, she never went to visit the lady again. She was frightened and ashamed. She felt bad about what she had done.

Probably all of us have had a similar experience about which we felt terribly guilty and ashamed. On the other hand, we've also experienced doing something right and good, then having a very positive feeling about ourselves. That leads to a better self-image, just as the opposite — doing things that are questionable or wrong in our own hearts and minds — will lead to a poorer self-image.

## Our Past

Our past, in part, determines who we are today. All of us are products of things that have happened to us during our growing up years. Although some psychologists over-emphasize the effects our childhood and life experiences have had on our lives, I believe we can better understand ourselves by looking at our pasts.

In *The Journal of Marriage and The Family*, authors Cooper,

Holman and Braithwaite said, "Those who report a high incidence of parental or family conflict are more likely to show . . . low self-esteem, even when this conflict occurred several years earlier."[3]

However, I do think it is important that we never let our past dictate how we think or behave in the present. Release from our past is one of the major principles that Jesus taught. He talked about turning pressure and pain into peace. "Come to Me," He said, "All who are weary and heavy-laden, and I will give you rest."[4] We don't have to be victims, but rather victors over our past.

There are other reasons for low self-image. In fact there are volumes of writing and research on the subject. But for the purposes of this book, I want to look now at how low self-esteem affects our relationships.

### Giving Up.

The first effect of low self-esteem can be just simply giving up. By that, I mean the person has so totally accepted the belief that he is inferior, he simply surrenders to it.

When I met Joan she was sitting up in a hospital bed. The friend who had introduced us was a psychiatrist and she was his patient. As we talked, I noticed how feeble and weak her movements were. It was also very obvious that she had a low self-image of herself in that she kept mentioning how people did not like her. "What's the use of trying?" she finally asked.

Joan — single and in her mid-twenties — was in the last stages of an emotional disease that is increasing in our country today — anorexia nervosa. She had convinced herself that she was fat in comparison to her friends and the movie stars she watched and read about. She also believed her weight was the reason she felt rejected by men and unaccepted by friends. She gave up trying to reach out to others and began punishing herself by going from 140 pounds to below 100, which was endangering her health. She starved herself, and when she did eat, she forced herself to vomit. She would listen to counseling, but would not act upon it. It seemed nothing and nobody could help. She had given up on herself. And she was dying of malnutrition.

Even though few of us go to the extent Joan did, once we surrender to negative thinking, we become less capable of developing and maintaining happy relationships. We push people away. In addition, we allow others to use and abuse us. (Sometimes we abuse ourselves too through drugs, alcohol or in even more severe ways as did Joan.) Most people do not enjoy spending time around negative, complaining, depressing people. Surrendering to futile hopelessness never has a happy ending.

**Afraid to Love.**

The second effect low self-esteem has on us is that we are afraid to give or receive love. Stanley Coppersmith in the book *The Antecedents of Self-Esteem* says:

> Clinicians observe that persons who are plagued by doubts of their worthiness can neither give nor receive love, apparently fearing that the exposure that comes with intimacy will reveal their inadequacies and cause them to be rejected. They thus avoid closeness in their relationships and feel isolated as a consequence.[5]

One of the better known Christian books written on relationships is John Powell's book, *Why Am I Afraid to Tell You Who I Am?* It deals with this fear of letting someone really get to know and love us. There is a capacity and yearning to love within all of us that we are afraid to release. We want to give our gift to others, but fear it will not be accepted. And that's due to our low self-esteem. Naturally, as long as we keep our love bottled inside (and the other person's love outside) relationships cannot grow.

"To the extent that a man lacks self-esteem," says Nathaniel Branden, "his consciousness is ruled by fear: Fear of reality, to which he feels inadequate; fear of the facts about himself which he has evaded or repressed."[6]

The fear (there's that word again) of losing someone often causes us to hold on more tightly, or to avoid subjects that would raise disagreements. The things we don't like about ourselves block our ability to express the real person inside when we are motivated by fear. It is like walking on eggshells.

If this is true of you, my suggestion is to relax. Let the burden of the relationship slide off your back. When you are yourself, you and your partner can enjoy each other more. Sooner or later you will have to break down the walls between you if the relationship is to have any chance to grow. Love and fear cannot grow together. So if, when you really have been yourself, the other person breaks up with you, remember that you probably would not have been happy anyway. You want to be loved for who you really are down deep inside. That kind of love is liberating.

### Jealousy.

Jealousy is the third way low self-esteem effects our relationships. It can be one of the most self-defeating and destructive elements in a dating relationship. It is also tied closely to the kind of fear discussed previously. In the article, "Jealousy, Romantic Love and Liking," (published in *Psychological Reports*), we read that a "recent belief concerning jealousy is the idea that it is the result of insecurity, low self-esteem . . . and lack of personal identity . . ."[7]

A person who is jealous is afraid of losing love, and in the process, usually does. Our fear of failure drives the other person away. "Jealousy," says Abraham Maslow (also quoted in the *Psychological Reports* article), "practically always breeds further rejection and deeper insecurity."[8]

### Criticism.

The fourth area where low self-esteem effects our relationships is the tendency to put others down. We attempt to make ourselves look better by being more critical and by refusing to see the best in others. In the book, *The Concept of Self,* Kenneth Gergen states,

> The person who feels inferior may not wish to admit to himself that others have positive attributes. To acknowledge others' superiority is to suffer through social comparison; to see them as inferior is to boost one's self-esteem. Through biased scanning one can always find shortcomings in others and in this way show himself that he is really not so bad after all.[9]

Being critical and picky all the time either drives the other person away . . . or makes the relationship very unsatisfying.

### Comparisons.

Fifth and last, low self-esteem causes us to make comparisons.

Craig was starting to like Beth. They had several fun dates. Although she was dating other guys, Beth asked Craig to come to a special party she was having. He had a good time, but felt inferior to Beth's friends. They were all popular people and he didn't feel that he belonged with that kind of crowd. As he compared himself with other guys Beth was dating, Craig got discouraged. "What does she see in me? I'm not her type. How can I compete?" So he never called her back although he wanted to many times.

Years later Beth married one of Craig's best friends. One evening when the three of them were having dinner together, they started talking about old times.

"Remember that party, when I invited you to be my date?"

Beth asked. "We had fun, but you never asked me out again. How come? I really liked you!"

Craig wanted to die.

Many dating relationships have failed because one of the pair felt inferior. When difficulties and differences developed — as they will in any relationship — the person compared himself with the competition and accepted defeat. Many times that happened to me. I gave up without a fight, or I never started in the first place. "She would never be interested in me." And sure enough, when I stopped pursuing the relationship, the woman generally would lose interest.

So, what are some solutions to our low self-esteem? How can we compensate for our weaknesses and develop our strengths?

**Accept Your Uniqueness.**

Remember that you were made in God's image and — as the saying goes — "He doesn't make junk." You are special to Him. With your strengths and weaknesses you are a valued person. Stop believing lies that would say otherwise. Dave Grant, a speaker and author, talks about the "radiation principle." What we radiate is what we attract. If we radiate confidence and honesty, we attract people with similar attributes. But if we radiate gloom and discouragement, we will also attract like-minded people . . . if we attract anyone at all.

We must realize that our intrinsic worth comes from our standing with God. If we are self-reliant, we depend upon ourselves or other people to give us a sense of worth and importance. But if we are dependent on Him, He fills us with Himself!

Joseph Aldrich, author of *Self Worth — How to Become More Loveable,* states it this way:

> If the whole world decided you were worthless, it would not change your essential value. Why? Because as a be-

liever you share both the image and nature of the unchanging God Himself. Your value is tied to Him.[10]

## Be Real.

Debbie knew very little about sports and could care less. But when she met Ron, a running back for the college football team, her attitude changed. She tried to change her interests to fit his. When they were together she acted as though she had been a big football fan for years. Instead of admitting her lack of knowledge and being honest about her real interests, she tried to fake it. Then came the big Saturday game. He played very well and was anxious to see what Debbie's impressions were of the game. When he came out of the locker room to meet her she said, "It was really exciting. But what was your number?" He left with a deflated ego and she didn't score any points.

Resist the temptation to try to be something you are not just to please someone. It is always good to learn new interests, but it is not good to pretend. Be real. And remember that your value and self-worth are *not* determined by others. Let God help you rise above circumstances and people's attitudes. He has made you worthy and precious.

## Reach Out to Others.

One of the fastest ways to climb out of low self-esteem is to focus on the needs of others instead of concentrating on your own needs. Dr. Larry W. Bailey, says,

> More intriguing . . . is the general thrust of the characteristics of the "happy" or "fulfilled" person. The focus is not on self-development or on self-growth or on any such self-orientation . . . furthermore, primary attention is repeatedly directed to attitudes toward and interactions with others — God, mankind in general, immediate associates. For Jesus, the focus of fulfillment is upon such apart-from-self concerns and involvements as empathy, responsiveness to others, active compassion, facilitat-

ing positive relationships and proper position in relationship to God. This is certainly a vivid contrast to most modern-day attempts to find "self" and generate a sense of self-fulfillment.[11]

Recently, I have been struggling with the meaning of life in general and my life in particular. If I try to solve these significant questions by focusing on my "self," I am guaranteed frustration and emptiness. Selfishness is never satisfying. But if I focus on a greater cause outside myself, it lifts me up and gives purpose to life.

The greatest cause to live for is Jesus Christ and His glory. He gave His life for us, "that they who live should no longer live for themselves, but for Him who died and rose again on their behalf."[12]

## Do What Is Right.

If you are currently and consistently doing something that you think might be wrong, find a close Christian friend, pastor or counselor to share it with. Get it off your chest. If they recommend that you stop doing it, then make every effort to do so. But, don't get down on yourself when you stumble. Instead, focus on doing and being that which would please God. Continue to share your struggles with your friend or counselor. Ask that person to pray for you, and commit yourself to doing those things which are right and pure. As a result, you will begin to feel the very best about yourself.

## Follow Wise Advice.

In Jesus' Sermon on the Mount, He said some pretty profound things which, when followed, can genuinely help one find the inner sense of peace and contentment that comes from doing right.

Here are some of the characteristics of people who have a good self-image according to Jesus in Matthew 5:3-10.

They are *poor in spirit,* humble before all-powerful God, constantly searching for wisdom, confident, but not conceited.

They are *mournful.* That means when they are down they are not knocked out because they are dependent on a loving heavenly Father. They are also sensitive to hurt and pain, others' as well as their own.

They are *gentle,* with a servant attitude toward others, understanding other people's sensitivities, and easy-going under pressure.

They *long for righteousness* and seek God's guidance. They are intolerant of wickedness and injustice and steadfast in personal morality.

They are *merciful,* forgiving wrongs done to them, compassionate toward people who have needs and responsive to requests for help.

They are *pure in heart,* truthful, sincere in their love for others, trustworthy, refusing to play games.

They are *peacemakers,* persistent in building harmony, friendly and cooperative even to disagreeable people.

They are *persecuted for righteousness,* resistent to harmful peer pressure, faithful to Jesus Christ regardless of the opposition and courageous when receiving abuse and mockery.

Sounds tough, doesn't it? These qualities seem impossible to possess. Well, they are — apart from God's transforming power.

Someone once told me that the Christian life was hard. I believed him at first, but I was mistaken. The Christian life is not hard to live at all. It is impossible! The only way to live like Christ is to have Him living in me. Then He will produce these qualities in me.

**Focus on God's Love.**

I'm convinced that if we could ever really see ourselves as

God sees us, we would never have trouble with low self-esteem again. He knew and cared for us even while we were in our mother's womb. He knows everything about us and nothing escapes His attention. He bends down to hear us when we talk to Him. When we admit our need for Him, He forgives our every sin and failure. He loves us as if we were His only child. And He promises, "I will never leave you or forsake you."[13]

# ABOLISHING THE 50/50 APPROACH

## Breakup Reason No. 4 — Selfishness

In relationships, self-centeredness can come out in very subtle ways.

I'm into antiques in a big way. I admire the beauty and craftsmanship of a well-built piece of antique furniture, especially pieces made of oak. In fact, in the past I've put much of my savings into antique furniture and knickknacks. Each year the value increases so I consider it to be an investment and an enjoyable hobby.

I will spend money on something that might look like junk to others. However, I can see the potential in it and know that once I have it refinished and fixed up a bit, it will be a beautiful piece of furniture.

But when I married Paula, antiques became a real bone of contention in our relationship. When we had a little extra money in the budget, my first inclination was to run out and look for more antiques.

I remember once at an auction I saw an antique lamp which was like one I'd been looking for for years. It had a beautiful, colored-glass shade. It was gorgeous.

I didn't know how much it would cost, but I guessed it would be expensive. I turned to Paula and asked her "Would you like to buy this lamp?"

She was hesitant. It seemed to her like too much money to spend on a lamp when she could go to Sears and get a very nice lamp for much less. Besides, she didn't think our home needed another lamp.

But I wanted it. As the auctioneer began, I became more frustrated. Finally I decided I was going to buy it anyway. An opportunity like this doesn't come along very often, at least that's what I told myself. The auctioneer started the bidding. The excitement intensified. I couldn't hold back. I raised my hand. "Going once, twice, sold."

Paula looked at me with horror in her eyes. "What in the world are you doing?" she asked. "Why did you do that?" It made absolutely no sense to her.

On the way home, with my wonderful, prized purchase, I was struck by the fact that it brought zero harmony to our relationship. Actually, it pulled us away from each other for just a bit. My selfish decision to buy that lamp was definitely a divisive thing.

As a consequence, I made a decision never to buy another antique until we both agreed on it together. As far as I am concerned, there is no antique on the face of the earth more important than my relationship with my wife. Even the rarest piece simply is not worth the conflicts that disharmony brings.

Some time later, I was really shocked — and excited — when Paula suggested we go to an antique auction. I tried hard not to show my surprise, but I about fell off my chair. She knew I would enjoy going to the auction, and suggested it for my sake. We agreed, though, that we would discuss thoroughly any purchases before we made them. We had learned a great deal about each other; about giving, sharing personal likes and dislikes and sacrificing for each other's happiness. We also learned how self-centeredness creates a real strain on a relationship.

### Self Centeredness

One of the primary reasons we date is to have fun and to

learn more about someone who helps us enjoy ourselves as well as enjoy life. We don't date to become unhappy. At least I've never heard anyone say, "I love to date this person because he makes me so miserable!" Yet misery is the state we find ourselves in many a time. Let's look at why.

Have you ever caught yourself thinking "Does the person I'm dating make me happy?" We all want to be fulfilled and satisfied and to find enjoyment.

But when you think about that question more seriously, it seems quite self-centered. "Do you make *me* happy?" That focuses on another person meeting our needs, on receiving rather than giving. We're all self-centered in many ways and it can make our relationships miserable. One of the funniest ways I've seen this portrayed is through photography. Suppose you're in a group photo. When the picture is developed who's the first person you look for in the photo? "Number One," that's who. Yourself!

And the more you look, the more you notice things you don't like about yourself in the picture. You say to your friend, "It's a terrible picture. I don't like it. My eyes are shut and I look horrible. Don't show it to anyone."

Why? Because none of us likes to be seen at less than the very best. Even if everyone in that photo is smiling and looking great, we look at our own image and decide the bad photo of ourselves far outweighs how good everyone else looks. The photo is going in the trash! We want very much to have "Number One" look good. That is being self-centered.

### Bargaining

Here's a way to help us see how being self-centered can affect our relationships: You begin to date a guy, and he really has it together. He's a leader type, confident, and certain that some day he will have a big, high-paying job. You also realize that he could provide you with the type of lifestyle you "would like to grow accustomed to." Your attitude toward him may be, "What a catch! He will give me a secure future."

But somewhere down the road, let's say he loses his job or becomes paralyzed from an auto accident. Would you still love him?

This applies to men too. They have a tendency to say, "Boy, does she get to me! She's fantastic! I'm definitely interested." What he's really saying is, "Because you turn me on, I'll love you." But what if she gets sick or loses her looks? Will you still love her? If not, you probably don't really *love* her at all.

Selfishness says, "If you do this, or give me this, then I will love you." But it never works on a lasting basis. Many professionals and books advocate a 50/50 partnership.[1] "*If* you do your part, I'll do mine." I've sat in on enough human sexuality and psychology classes to realize how prominent this philosophy is. It all sounds so plausible, but it contains a fatal flaw.

Don Meredith, in his book *Becoming One*, deals with this issue.

> Why, when it seems to make so much sense, is the meet-me-halfway concept dangerous? It draws the couples' eyes to each other's *performance*, and no one is perfect, or performs correctly all the time. Further, it actually promotes *independence:* You do your job; I'll do mine. Once we start focusing on one another's performance, we begin to feel rejection and hurt.[2]

In light of all the counseling I have done with dating couples, I am convinced this kind of bargaining will never work. The reason is that you can never be sure the other person is doing as much as they should. "Hey, look at what I do for you, and then look at what I get in return. It's not enough! I deserve a lot more."

The 50/50 relationship produces insecurity and confusion. "Does he love me enough?" "Is she giving as much as I am to this relationship?" "If I stop doing my part, will he stop loving me?"

## Comparisons

Focusing on ourselves and our own desires for happiness, produces another attitude that often splits couples apart. It is comparison: selfishly desiring what someone else has.

There are lots of people of the opposite sex who are attractive to us and it can be fun — and even healthy — to "play the field." But the comparison I'm talking about occurs after you have been dating someone for a while. As you are developing a relationship, when another person attracts your attention, how do you react?

Let's say you have gone to a party, for example, with your boyfriend. You're standing there talking and munching on snacks when in walks Jill with her boyfriend. You look at her boyfriend, then at yours, and you think, "How did she ever get him? What does she have that I don't have?"

We guys do the same thing. But the problem is that what initially attracts us to another person is the external or the positive side of that person. We forget she has a negative side too . . . and she can't make us totally happy either.

According to researchers Stan Albrecht and Phillip Kunz,
Almost all persons have a tendency to put on their best front in public and not reveal those important negative things that occur in their private relationships. Thus, the comparison level that many couples use when they compare their own relationship is an artificial comparison level. They measure themselves against the public mask of others. Each person knows his or her private life and the problems that exist there, but tends to see only the better side of others.[3]

When you're not happy within yourself, you may look for someone "out there" to meet those happiness needs. Very soon, you will discover that each new dating partner has weaknesses, also, though they may be in different areas. No one is perfect, including you. Satisfaction comes when two imperfect people work together to build a realistic relationship.

Selfishly desiring what doesn't belong to you does not automatically stop once you are married. One of my college professors was a psychiatrist. I learned many tremendous things from this man. During his professional career he counseled hundreds of couples. A certain woman began to come to his office for counseling, and, over several months time, he started comparing her to his wife. Eventually, he became involved with this woman who seemed to understand him in a special way and added "electricity" to his life.

I knew his family well. It hurt terribly to see that slowly but surely this man, who knew how to counsel others, could no longer counsel himself. He ended up destroying his marriage and devastating his wife and two children.

He was looking for someone else to make him happy. The sad thing is, he is still unhappy today. Pursuing selfish interests ultimately leaves us feeling miserable and empty.

"A hunger for deeper personal relationships," says Daniel Yankelovich, "shows up in our research finding as a growing conviction that a me-first, satisfy-all-my-desires attitude leads to relationships that are superficial, transitory and ultimately unsatisfying."[4]

Even if we do finally find one person to love and settle down with, we soon discover that our desire to have more is very much alive. The more deeply involved we become with someone, the more our selfishness is exposed. We want our own way. To get it, we argue, pout, demand, manipulate and scheme. Yet after we get it, the happiness is fleeting. It is like clutching a fist full of sand, only to have the sand slide between our fingers and fall to the ground.

## A New Heart

What we need is a change — not of relationships, but of heart. The ancient prophet Ezekiel wrote that God would "give you a new heart and put a new spirit within you; and . . . remove the heart of stone from your flesh and give you a heart of flesh."[5]

The stone heart refers to the stubborn streak within each of us. Self-reliance and self-centeredness plagues us all. We want "me-first" in our lives. We are hesitant and even fearful to let anyone, including God, have a more important place than ourselves.

I used to love going fishing with my Dad on the coasts of southern New Jersey. After a long, hot day on the rented boat, we would drive up the interstate highway to our home in the northern part of the state.

"Dad, would you let me drive?" I'd plead. Because I was only 12 years old he would hesitate. But with my usual persistence, he gave in. As I sat in his lap, my feet unable to touch the gas pedal, I drove the car as if I owned the road.

One day as I was driving we were coming to an important intersection. Dad wanted to go right and I wanted to go left. A struggle took place. I was pretty strong. Dad finally yanked the steering wheel and we went right.

Two people cannot drive a car in two different directions at the same time. Someone has to be in control. In the same manner just as that car had two people wanting to do it their way, within us all there's a similar struggle. Ezekiel called it the heart of stone and the heart of flesh. What kind of heart controls your life, heart of stone or a heart of flesh?

The heart of stone is our old self-centered nature. It is what we were born with and what has dominated our lives. A stone is hard, cold and dead. Old "Number One" wants his own way. "I have a right to be happy." What we really mean is "I have a right to run my life the way I want." Since we are imperfect, self-centered and fallible, our heart of stone leads us to harmful consequences including broken relationships and even separation from God and His vibrant love.

On the other hand, a heart of flesh is produced in our lives when, as the Lord says ". . . I will put My Spirit within you and cause you to walk in My statutes . . ."[6] In this passage, flesh is a symbol of warmth and softness. In this condition we are connected to the personal, loving God of the universe. His power captivates our lives and His love motivates us to be dependent upon Him for everything in life — including happiness.

"Your heavenly Father knows that you need all these things," exclaims Jesus. "But seek first His kingdom and His righteousness; and *all* these things shall be added to you."[7] Happiness is not the right target. It is only the by-product of hitting the bullseye of God's purposes. The same is true in our relationships. When we focus on others first, people sense our love and caring.

## To Find Love

Dr. James Lynch, scientific director of the Psychophysiological Clinic of Maryland School of Medicine, is quoted as describing a simple and yet profound solution: "Basically, if you want to find love, you've got to give love. That sounds trite, but it's true. That tenet is often difficult to practice in today's society, where deep relationships are hard to establish and easy, impersonal contacts are more common."[8]

Contrary to all of our natural instincts, true fulfillment and happiness come from giving of ourselves. It starts inside when we go from a stone heart to a heart of flesh. As the Lord helps remove selfishness, He also helps us show love toward others.

Dr. Larry Bailey, a professor of psychology, writes,
> Perhaps more intriguing is the general thrust of the characteristics of the "happy" or "fulfilled" person. The focus is *not* on self-development or on self-growth or any such self-orientation. For Jesus the focus of fulfillment is upon such apart-from-self concerns and involvements as empathy, responsiveness to others, active compassion, facilitating positive relationships, and a proper position in relationship to God.[9]

Self-centeredness can never bring us the kind of relationships we want. Jesus said, ". . . It is more blessed to give than to receive."[10] Jesus was not referring to money at all in that passage. He was talking about giving of our *selves* to others. When you give selflessly of your time, love and consideration to another you will receive beautifully in return. God will bless a giving heart. He sure taught me that through the antique lamp episode.

Whether you are in a dating relationship or not, seek to build people up and to give of yourself rather than merely to take. Friendships are based on trust and mutual sharing of lives. In whatever stage your relationship is, take an interest in the person — his ideas and feelings. Avoid the 50/50 attitude and learn to give 100%.

# ENJOYING
# SEXUAL SANITY

## Breakup Reason No. 5 — Sexual Burnout

I decided to celebrate! My birthday had passed, but there had been no opportunity to do something special because I had been out of town on a speaking trip. When I finally returned home, my date and I went out to an elegant restaurant for a one-time-a-year expensive dinner. A night to remember.

But it ended up being a night of horror. Oh sure, the dinner was delicious and the restaurant had a long French name I couldn't pronounce. However, after returning home and going to bed, I woke up at 2 A.M. with severe abdominal pain. It was one of those times I was afraid I was going to die and yet afraid I wouldn't die. I lay there, thinking the pain would subside, but it intensified. With great agony and effort I stumbled into my roommate Tim's room and blurted out, "Take me to the hospital!"

I had just made it to the bathroom when my stomach erupted the expensive meal. Tim hurriedly wrapped some clothes around me and rushed me to the hospital downtown where the doctors accomplished the task of calming both me and my stomach.

The evening had started out so enjoyably and had ended so miserably. The meal had packed a surprise. I loved the food, but it made me miserable. Sex can pack a surprise, too.

I was speaking at a conference and afterward George asked if we could talk alone. He was concerned about his relationship with his girlfriend.

"Why do I feel depressed?" He asked. "I really like her, but something is disturbing me. I should be happy, but I'm not."

It was an all-too-familiar story. They couldn't be together enough at the beginning. Fun and excitement filled their lives as they spent hours talking about every imaginable subject. Their affection had led to touching, then to hugs and ultimately lots more. It seemed to them so natural to express their love in bed. But the thrill started to change to doubts. They began arguing more than usual. Hurt feelings and disappointments came. He said they were still dating, but that now it was more out of habit than enjoyment.

That was George's story, but he is only one of many. Today there are thousands of surprised couples. Sexual freedom has brought along its complications and couples are discovering that "free love" isn't free.

In a recent issue of *Psychology Today* an article title, in big black letters across two pages, read "The Broken Promises of the Sexual Revolution." It really caught my eye. After all, this wasn't in a religious magazine but rather a respected secular publication which reflects much of today's thinking.

In the article, author Peter Marin says:

> What most of us currently seem to believe is that once restraints are removed from human behavior, "nature" simply asserts itself, like water filling an empty space. We forget that we bring with us, into any kind of freedom, the baggage of the past, our internalized cultural limits and weaknesses. Thus freedom — in this case sexual freedom — increases choice, but it guarantees nothing, delivers nothing. To the extent that it diversifies and expands experience, it also diversifies and multiplies the pain that accompanies experience, the kinds of errors that we make, the kinds of harm that we can do to one another.[1]

Indeed, free love isn't really free. Yet we continue being

bombarded with its "promises" from most movies, TV, magazines and sometimes even our friends. We hear:

"If it feels good, it's okay."

"Sex is the greatest experience."

"Everybody is doing it."

"Live for today, don't worry about tomorrow."

"Virginity is old-fashioned."

With all the sexual freedom, you would think that people would be much happier, that misery would be replaced by joy. But that hasn't happened.

Everywhere I speak, people want to talk about their needs. And their greatest need is to find real love. Unfortunately, many of these people still have not learned that sex and love are not the same.

Dr. Norman Wright, counselor and psychologist, succinctly expresses the differences in the chart on the next page.[2]

Still, in the last decade we have seen sex come boldly out of the bedroom, onto the TV and into the classrooms. Today it is accepted — and sometimes even expected — that single women sleep with the men they date.[3] And, according to Dr. Gabrielle Brown, "The prevailing male lesson is that masculinity is sexual, and performance and equipment count for almost the whole ball game."[4]

Why do we get sexually involved in the first place? There are a lot of reasons, but here are the most prevalent.

**Natural Drives.**

Romance is the spark that lights up your relationship. When you want to express love and tenderness, touching seems only natural. But once you begin, the power of sexual urges drives the two of you to go further — maybe beyond what you had intended. But at the time, who cares about tomorrow? As the song goes, "Tonight is all we have so let's love each other."

**LOVE . . .**

...is a process; you must go through it to understand what it is.

...is a learned operation; you must learn what to do through first having been loved and cared for by someone.

...requires constant attention.

...experiences slow growth — takes time to develop and evolve.

...is deepened by creative thinking.

...is many small behavior changes that bring about good feelings.

...is an act of will with or without good feelings — sometimes "don't feel like it."

...involves the respect of the person to develop.

...is lots of warm laughter.

...requires knowing how to thoughtfully interact, to talk, to develop interesting conversations.

...develops in depth to sustain the relationship, involves much effort, where eventually real happiness is to be found.

**SEX . . .**

...is static; you have some idea of what it is like prior to going through it.

...is known naturally; you know instinctively what to do.

...takes no effort.

...is very fast — needs no time to develop.

...is controlled mostly by feel — that is, responding to stimuli.

...is one big feeling brought about by one big behavior.

...is an act of will — you feel like it.

...does not require the respect of the person.

...is little or no laughter.

...requires little or no talking.

...promises permanent relationship but never happens, can't sustain relationship, forever feature is an illusion.

**Loneliness.**

In a national survey of over 3,000 singles, over 85% said they were lonely.[5] It is the number one problem that single adults face. To have someone to share your life with seems the ideal way to find companionship. But when people are in a hurry and can't wait to develop an in-depth togetherness, sex is the easy way.

Stephen C. Board quotes Dr. Mary Stewart, assistant professor of psychology, as saying,

> I began to see that the need to be always in a sexual relationship with someone . . . was a desperate fight against a rarely admitted loneliness and isolation. It was the best (or only) way I knew how to approximate some reassurance that somehow, for a little while anyway, there was a semblance of commitment, caring and communication. It was always the same way: a fellow and I would start out with a tremendous euphoric closeness which sooner or later became empty and ritualized. We would go along playing the game for a while, but finally one or the other of us would pull out, determined that next time it would be different. It never was.[6]

**Peer Pressure.**

Many a person today is embarrassed to admit being a virgin. Most people don't talk about it without apologizing. Intercourse has become the rite of passage to manhood or womanhood. By graduation from high school, 60% of the men and 40% of the women have had pre-marital sex. By the end of college, the numbers have increased to 80% of the men and 65% of the women having become sexually active. In 1982, 188,000 college freshmen were asked, "Is it right for people who like each other to have sex?" Over 48% of the students said yes.[7]

Dr. Richard V. Lee of Children's Hospital of Buffalo (NY) is quoted in *Families* magazine as contending that the youth rebellion against the old morality has transformed sex into an ideology "as dictatorial and cruel as Victorian prudery. It has used easier contraception, legal abortion and surer therapeutic methods for venereal disease as arguments to make virginity irrelevant. It refuses to accept virginity as a reasonable way of life. In short, it allows no choice. Our sexual liberation does not include the freedom to say no."[8]

Both men and women suffer from the pressure. In *Families,* November, 1981, a University of Arizona student expressed her disappointment.

"I told myself that I was going to stay a virgin until I was married." But in college, she found the pressures more than she could resist. "I met somebody I loved enough to give up my virginity for. But the whole time we made love the TV was on. And when it was over, he just switched channels and lit up a joint. God, was I angry! Here I had made the ultimate sacrifice and he didn't care. I was hoping through the whole thing that he'd say, 'I love you.' "[9]

We have discussed in previous chapters several reasons dating couples have difficulty and may break up. After counseling hundreds of people I am convinced that one of the primary reasons relationships split apart is because of sexual burnout. Both men and women will place the blame for the final goodbyes on arguments, broken promises, incompatibilities and other legitimate tensions, when many times the underlying sexual involvement is what started the downhill spiral. It is hard to recognize it and even more difficult to admit it. The myth of sexual freedom dies hard.

Have you ever spent hours in a long make-out session, and then not wanted to see the person in the morning? It seemed right the night before — the warmth and thrill of sexual passion. But the next day is a different story.

Your friends, or the media, may portray the night of passion as normal and expected for a couple. But no one ever talks about the let-down feelings of the morning after. How does sexual involvement destroy dating relationships?

For one thing, it increases loneliness. That seems contradictory doesn't it? Someone thinks enough of you to want to be physically close but that doesn't take away the loneliness. In the book, *Singles: The New Americans,* a Seattle woman shares this, a typical, single-adult response:

> I often go to a bar I like, out of loneliness. I want some warm, loving company. When I pick up a man though and make love with him, the opposite happens. I feel more lonely than before.[10]

In the same book we also read, "Women often describe casual sex as 'lonely' . . . men are more inclined to characterize it as 'meaningless' or 'empty.' "[11]

Love and good sex are both built on knowledge, personal understanding and a commitment to each other. It goes beyond superficiality. Dr. James Dobson writes,

> Real love, in contrast to popular notions, is an expression of the deepest appreciation for another human being; it is an intense awareness of his or her needs and longings for the past, present and future. It is unselfish and giving and caring. And believe me these are not attitudes one "falls" into at first sight, as though he were tumbling into a ditch.[12]

Without trust and devotion, passion can produce a kind of superficial caring. But sex was created by God to be the culmination of the process of bringing two lives together so that they can become a cohesive unit. This oneness develops through growing harmony and companionship. "Real intimacy" states Erik Erikson, "includes the capacity to commit yourself to relationships that may demand sacrifice and compromise. The basic strength of young adulthood is having a mutual, mature devotion."[13]

The length of time a couple has been dating is not a good measure of their depth of oneness. I have met couples who have been dating for over a year and still lack unity. They are two individuals who are spending time together, but who are going in different directions.

Dr. C. Roy Fowler, Executive Director, Academy of Family Mediators, when asked about the sexual revolution, replied:

> Apparently, the experience has rarely matched the promise. The growing disillusionment with sexual freedom is based on non-fulfillment felt by the participants. Shooting the rapids of life's physical and psychic flow has caught too many persons in an endless maelstrom of meaningless relationships, or left them washed up and exhausted on the beaches of loneliness.[14]

Another way in which sexual involvement destroys dating relationships is by undermining intimacy. There is physical closeness, but the other parts of a person's life are often not involved. Even when two people consent to make love, it does not mean intimacy is achieved. A person is much more than a body and sex organs. Intercourse is more than a physical act. It involves the whole being, including the spiritual aspect. To use each other simply for the pursuit of pleasure leaves inevitable emotional scars.

Rollo May has said, "For human beings, the more powerful need is not for sex per se, but for relationships, intimacy, acceptance and affirmation."[15]

Gabrielle Brown also says in *The New Celibacy:*

> Sex is, in fact, often used as an excuse for actually avoiding intimacy. If one is afraid of the surrender required for growing intimacy, sex can be used as a cover for that fear. But at the same time that sex may be used as an escape from the threat of intimacy, it is also the only way many people know to be intimate. So what may happen is that the deep yearnings of two people to

grow closer are frustrated by this one limited choice of love communication on which they depend for fulfillment and growth of intimacy.[16]

The insecurity of being loved only physically and not being known and accepted totally and completely is devastating.

A third way a dating relationship is destroyed by sexual involvement is that it inevitably produces guilt.

"I don't feel guilty," a woman told Paula, my wife. "My boyfriend and I sleep together and it's okay."

"It doesn't matter," Paula answered, "whether you feel guilty or not. According to God's law you are guilty."

If someone is caught stealing, the judge doesn't ask if that person *feels* guilty. That doesn't matter. The law has been broken and the sentence is determined by what was done, not by how the person feels.

Deep inside each person is a moral code. The Bible says that God's law is written on the heart of each person.[17] Since the beginning of man's existence on this earth, God has implanted His righteous principles into the very fiber of each one of us.

I want to be very clear about this point. God did not give moral laws to hurt us or to make us miserable. In fact, He gave them to protect us and to give us satisfaction.

Governments set up traffic laws to protect us. For example, they dictate on which side of the road a person can drive a car. Suppose there were no such laws. The highways would be utterly chaotic and dangerous.

And when we disobey such laws, moral or governmental, guilt is the deep, nagging result.

Dean shared his deeply emotional experience with me. He had met Terri at the big downtown church. They had similar interests and spent many hours together. He just knew that this time it would be different because he was definitely interested in her.

They enjoyed touching and hugging. One spring evening as they sat in the car at a romantic spot just outside of town, his desire for her was more than he could contain. Their passion seemed to light up the night sky as all his reasoning for minimal sexual contact melted away.

No, they didn't go all the way, but they went further than they had ever gone before. After his heartbeat returned to normal, the uneasy feelings began. Sure, it was exciting. He was a red-blooded, American male. But he began to feel empty and guilty. As he held her in his arms under the night sky, he began to realize he was doing so more out of a sense of duty than because he genuinely cared.

They couldn't get back to her house fast enough for him. He gave her a quick kiss and drove home — frustrated and lonely. According to the music he listened to in the car, he was supposed to feel elated. But he was both disgusted with himself and disappointed in her. All he could think of was, "Here I go again! Guilty and sorry."

The next Saturday night Dean and Terri parked at the same spot and had the same results. Only this time, the guilt wasn't so overwhelming. But they didn't talk much as their physical desires began to consume them. They both suppressed their guilt feelings, being careful never to discuss what they both knew was wrong.

Dean's heart began to grow cold toward Terri as they communicated less and less and argued more and more. It seemed like as long as they were making out everything was okay. But during the rest of the time they got on each other's nerves.

When the end finally came a few months later, they had never admitted to each other the guilt which drove a wedge between them.

Guilt separates people and can even affect personalities.

One doctor told me that over half of the hospital beds in America are occupied by the mentally ill or people with emotionally based physical problems. And according to many reports the number one reason for these problems is guilt. So it affects both our relationships and us as individuals.

Besides increasing loneliness, undermining intimacy and producing guilt, sexual involvement in a dating relationship inhibits communication.

We've already spent an entire chapter discussing communication. But it bears repeating. Have you ever noticed that the more petting you do, the less talking there is? As the physical increases, meaningful conversation decreases. And no strong relationship can exist without regular, healthy, in-depth conversation.

"Whoever commits sin," Jesus proclaims, "is a slave to sin."[18] We become enslaved to our passions. The results are seen in the frustrations and arguments that split people apart.

But God did not intend for sex to split people apart. In fact, He created sex to be the superglue that helps bond marriage relationships together. The emotional and mental tie between the two when they marry is so strong that God says they are actually one flesh — a unit. "For this cause a man shall leave his father and his mother, and shall cleave to his wife; and they shall become one flesh."[19] The word "cleave" reflects the basic meaning of joining to one another in loyalty and devotion. The word occurs sixty times in the Hebrew Old Testament and is even used to show how we are to cling to the Lord.[20] That same word in modern Hebrew means "glue." What a beautiful description of love — to stick to someone in loyalty and devotion.

Sexual involvement and intercourse are reserved for marriage — not because God doesn't want us to enjoy each other, but because He wants to give us the security of a life-long love relationship.

We are to cleave to God and when He unites us with another person in marriage, we are to cleave to that person like none other in life.

"The primary factor," writes Josh McDowell, "is the unity factor. It's to give a man and a woman 'one-fleshness' — an experience in the physical realm which illustrates the intensity of the spiritual relationship a man or woman has with God when he or she is reborn through Jesus Christ."[21]

Another major consequence of premarital sexual involvement is that it damages our most important relationship of all, that being our relationship with our Creator. Let's test this right now: When you are indulging in sexual activity, do you enjoy praying?

When Dean was involved with Terri, he didn't want to talk to God. He was afraid that God might convict him of something he "enjoyed" doing. It also became harder to study the Bible as his heart grew increasingly colder toward the Lord.

Isn't it interesting how we try to fake people out? We put up a pious false front until it crumbles. And in the process, we think God is fooled along with everyone else. Think again.

"But there is nothing covered up," Jesus said "that will not be revealed, and hidden that will not be known. Accordingly whatever you have said in the dark shall be heard in the light, and what you have whispered in the inner rooms shall be proclaimed upon the housetops."[22]

All the while Dean was dating Terri, he knew that God saw him. He tried to hide. He rationalized. "We love each other. It's okay. Besides we haven't had intercourse."

But they had no deep commitment toward each other. God is not against sex. He is against the mutual exploitation and defrauding which robs us of the joy of life.[23]

His holy light exposes our sin. We feel guilty because we

are guilty, not just of sexual sins, but of self-centeredness. In the same instant, God offers the solution. Jesus never sinned, but He died to cleanse our sins and to clear our consciences. As a result, we can walk in the light and not be fearful of God. The slate is wiped clean. "If we confess our sins," the apostle John writes, "He is faithful and righteous to forgive us our sins and to cleanse us from all unrighteousness."[24]

Dean shared with me that he finally got tired of hiding and trying to run away from the Lord. The Holy Spirit convicted him of his unholiness and rationalization. One night he poured out his heart to God about his disobedience in having broken sexual barriers with Terri. He desperately wanted forgiveness and the pleasure of openness with the Lord, and God met his need. God's joy flooded Dean's heart as he humbled himself before Him.

John White, in his excellent book, *Eros Defiled,* expresses these thoughts beautifully.

> The experience of freedom has to do with being loved and loving. God designed you because He loved you. His purposes for you are an expression of His love to you. And as you respond in love to His commands (about sex or anything else) you are set free, free to be and to do what both you and God want. The more completely you are enslaved in love to His blessed will, the freer you will discover yourself to be.[25]

If you are hiding from God, reach out to receive His forgiveness and freedom.

# A

## LASTING

## LOVE

# COMMITMENT:
# THE FORGOTTEN KEY

One day a pig and a chicken were walking down the road together, looking for a place to eat breakfast. After awhile, they saw a large sign in front of a restaurant which read "Special Today. Ham and Eggs." The chicken said, "Hey, this looks like a great breakfast!" The pig snorted, "No way. Eggs from a chicken are a contribution. But ham from a pig is a total commitment."

Many of us are like the chicken, giving only a very small part of ourselves to a relationship. But lasting relationships require much more.

Back in my college days, several of my classmates and I were discussing what to do for an assigned sociology class project. We decided to visit a home for delinquent boys, and we asked Dr. Glover, our professor, to come with us.

To our disappointment she responded, "I would like to, but I have to do something more important." Since we enjoyed her classes so much, we persisted. We asked her again but she responded, "No, I have to visit someone at the hospital." We all knew that the hospital she named was a mental hospital, so she had our attention. "Are you going to do some counseling?" we asked. "No," she replied, "I'm going to visit my husband."

We were shocked. Although we knew she had been married over 20 years, we did not know of her husband's condition. After she explained the situation briefly, one of my friends blurted out, "If he's that sick, why don't you get a divorce?" I'll never forget her answer: "Because, he's my husband!" She needed to give no other explanation. She had committed herself to be his wife "until death do you part."

With over 1.1 million divorces per year, one doesn't hear of too many examples like this. People "jump ship" far too quickly and for much more insignificant reasons than having a mate in a mental institution.

Erich Fromm, the world-famous psychoanalyst, wrote these challenging thoughts in his book *The Art of Loving:*

> To love means to commit oneself without guarantee, to give oneself completely in the hope that our love will produce love in the loved person. Love is an act of faith and whoever is of little faith is also of little love.[1]

The word "commitment" is almost a foreign word to us. Daniel Yankelovich states that, when an Associated Press/NBC poll asked Americans in 1978 whether they thought "most couples getting married today expect to remain married for the rest of their lives," a 60 percent majority said no.[2] Today, that figure would probably be higher. While marriages are dissolving at alarming rates, the number of unmarried couples living together — usually involving little or no commitment — has risen dramatically. According to *U.S. News and World Report,* "The Census Bureau estimates that the number of couples involved in such relationships soared from 523,000 in 1970 to 1.9 million in 1982."[3] A recent survey among single adults, shows approximately one half of all single men and a third of all single women have at one time or another lived with a member of the opposite sex.[4]

Today marriage and commitment are taken lightly.

Recently, I read an interesting newspaper story. American screen idol Ava Gardner said in an interview that she would have given up her career in a minute in exchange for a long, happy marriage. She grew up hoping to find "one good man I could love and marry and cook for and make a home for, who would stick around for the rest of my life. I have never found him."[5] She is now over 60 years old and has been married 3 times, all to very prominent men: Mickey Rooney, famous actor; Artie Shaw, famous musician; and Frank Sinatra, famous entertainer. Riches and fame have not satisfied her, whereas some of the more simple basics of life might have. Now, looking back on her life she regrets the shallow way she pursued relationships.

What does all this have to do with dating? A lot. Many of the behavioral patterns established during our dating years follow us into marriage. Let's take a look at some of the reasons we find it hard to be committed in a relationship.

**A Mind Set.**

When I was a young boy, Dad always made me finish whatever job I started. But unfortunately as an adult I am a procrastinator and an impetuous person. I often just get going on one project then leave to start another. I find myself with many unfinished jobs around the house at one time.

Some of us have that same attitude in our relationships. Sometimes it appears the all-American attitude is "Get in there and quit." Like many of the jobs we have started during our lives, relationships get too hard or too difficult to finish. Our dads are no longer beside us to see that we finish what we start. Many of us have a hard time sticking to anything for a long time. So, unfortunately, in our relationships we find it easier to walk away and start over than to "gut it out," searching for solutions and compatibility.

Of course, you will have opportunities to date more than one person, and that is fine. But if you find yourself skipping from person to person due to small disagreements, poor communication, fickle emotions or false assumptions, no matter what your reason, you are denying yourself the opportunities to develop healthy, in-depth relationships.

**Past Pain.**

You may have had one or more breakups in the past. If so, the pain involved may have been great, and you say to yourself, "Never again. I've learned my lesson." We protect ourselves and withdraw in the fear that we may get hurt again. Many of us have the attitude, "It just doesn't pay to get too involved or committed." But what we don't understand is that risk is a part of love. C.S. Lewis has a powerful thought in his book, *The Four Loves:*

> To love at all is to be vulnerable. Love anything, and your heart will certainly be wrung and possibly be broken. If you want to make sure of keeping it intact, you must give your heart to no one, not even to an animal. Wrap it carefully around with hobbies and little luxuries; avoid all entanglements. Lock it up safe in the casket or coffin of your selfishness. But in that casket — safe, dark, motionless, airless — it will change. It will not be broken; it will become unbreakable, impenetrable, irredeemable.
>
> The alternative to tragedy, or at least to the risk of tragedy, is damnation. The only place outside heaven where you can be perfectly safe from all the dangers and perturbations of love is Hell.[6]

**Societal Attitudes.**

When I played football in high school, the locker room was the place to hear guys talk about their exploits with women. To many of the men it didn't matter what the girl was like as long as she gave in to their advances. It was often conquer, break up, and move on to the next conquest.

Women can be just as shallow. It is not terribly uncommon for a woman to express to a friend her delight in the conquest of the men in her life.

It's hard to get away from the flippant attitudes people have about the opposite sex. Soap operas intrigue millions daily with blatant affairs and torrid romances. Movies, books, magazines and TV subtlely, and sometimes not so subtlely, dwell on the superficial, sensual aspects of a relationship.

Have you ever noticed, on the news stand, that magazine articles which talk about sexual relationships often refer to the person of the opposite sex as a "lover" or "partner"? Seldom is the reference made to "husband" or "wife." Of course not, there is no need to get a marriage license for a weekend fling or for a "new romance" according to those writers.

Our friends send us messages, also. An article in *Psychology Today* stated, "Social pressure is one of the primary reasons for people to give in, or relapse on commitments they've made. . . . Friends — the kind of people we surround ourselves with — really make a difference."[7]

All these messages bombard us with the attitude that it's okay to live out our temporary fantasies without the faintest notion of long term caring or sensitivity to the other person's deep needs. But too often the consequences of our self-centered behavior are neither admitted or discussed.

**Quest for Success.**

A generation or so ago, the entire family was required to work together for survival. Dad needed Mom and the kids to help on the farm or in the family business. But today — with our lives made easier, with many women working on their own and the entire family going in so many different directions — we no longer need each other to survive. So rather than being concerned with the welfare of others, we are primarily concerned with our own. We live in a family of strangers — each person in his own little world.

In addition, according to sociologist Tony Campolo in a *Solo* magazine interview, "Our society's primary determination of success today is money and power."[8] Those of us who believe that are consumed with the desire to acquire wealth (and things) as well as status and position. In order to do this, we don't dare make many commitments to those who might hold us back. In fact, Campolo explained that one of the reasons we make fewer commitments today is that we've learned a valuable lesson. We can actually acquire more wealth and power when we don't think about anyone else but ourselves. So off we go on the quest to success, only to find a selfish, empty end. This craving for success is more important to many of us than the desire for developing the relationships we have established. Eventually the result may well be an explosion.

If your girlfriend called to tell you she just smashed up your new B.M.W., what would your immediate reaction be? "Are you hurt?" or "What happened to the car?"

When you are under emotional stress on your job, do you and your partner argue more and put each other down?

Would you rather read the business magazine than discuss the misunderstanding which has both you and your partner upset?

In these unguarded moments our hidden motives bubble to the surface. Too many people have become successful in their careers but have destroyed their relationships or lost their families. If children are involved, they are usually the ones who pay the terrible price of success. John Powell says, "It is a law of human life, as certain as gravity: To live fully, we must learn to *use* things and *love* people . . . not *love* things and *use* people. . ."[9]

**Unwillingness to Pay the Price.**

The goal is happiness. We want the "good life." Self-denial and sacrifice are not part of the plan. We want the freedom to attain satisfaction, but do not want to pay the price.

"Self-denial has lost much of its normative appeal," says Daniel Yankelovich, author of *New Rules.* He adds:

> If I have a duty to myself, satisfying rather than denying, the self becomes the ascendent norm. A traditional family life is no longer the prime symbol of respectability. Conversely, you no longer lose your respectability if you are divorced, choose to live alone, refuse to have children or belong to a household in which both spouses work. [10]

Have you ever overheard a conversation that caught and held your attention? As I was sitting in a restaurant, waiting for my food, I happened to hear two older men at a nearby table. One was bemoaning his recent divorce.

"I can't understand her," he lamented. "All these years I have worked hard to build a business, and now she leaves me. How could she do it? I gave her everything, a gorgeous house and an expensive car." I thought, *How blind. Didn't he realize that giving someone a house and a car is easier than giving himself, but he is what she wanted?* Material things do not really satisfy the heart for very long.

Andre Bustanoby, a Washington, D.C., counselor, says that the only way we can find the kind of deep friendship and intimacy we are looking for is through commitment. But to make a commitment requires that we both pay a price and carry a burden. Few of us are willing to do that. [11]

For example, men, do you respect her "no" because you are more concerned about her feelings than your own desires?

Women, do you consider his budget concerns and willingly accept a less expensive evening because you are more interested in his concerns than your own desires?

Do you encourage each other to do your very best in school or on the job, even if that means sacrificing some of the time you would like to spend together?

The sacrifice required for commitment is costly, but it is the price which has to be paid in order to establish meaningful re-lationships. If we continue trying to meet our needs through less personally costly means, all we will find is disillusionment and disappointment.

Before we go on, I'd like us to see one thing in perspective. I do not believe that every person should get married. Several of my close friends are single. Most of them enjoy dating but prob-ably will choose to marry some day. However, I would never pressure them to marry. During my 42 years of being single, too many people made me feel like a second-class citizen because I was single. I enjoyed those years with their special struggles and pleasures. There are tremendous advantages in being single.

Even if you have no desire to get married, you still need to learn the practical, valuable ways to build close friendships, as discussed in this book. If you do plan to get married, it is imper-ative you learn to develop these qualities. Surveys show that 70 percent of Americans now recognize that while they have many acquaintances they have few close friends, and they see this as a serious void in their lives.[12] We can all improve our friendship building skills.

**My Search for Commitment.**

During my college days, I struggled with a lot of problems in my life. After my breakup with Amy — plus other disappoint-ments along the way — I began wondering if I could count on anyone or anything. Girlfriends brought on heartbreak, and other people kept disappointing me. Life was so confusing.

I had become a Christian at the age of seven at a children's Bible club and had sat in a pew nearly every Sunday since. But as the years passed, I became more and more frustrated as I tried to copy the dynamic life portrayed in the Bible. I just could not live it! Sometimes I could fake people out — and even fooled myself. But the consistent love and strength needed to cope with everyday situations just was not there. Who wanted to be committed to mediocrity? Not me. But what alternative did I have?

I searched for people in whom I could find the right answers and whom I could pattern my life after. But couldn't find anyone I wanted to be like. I wanted vitality, power and lasting love. Where could I find all that? I almost gave up.

One day, while I was sitting in my dorm room at college, it suddenly hit me. People have failed — but Jesus hasn't, and He never will! His love for individuals is still being talked about today, nineteen centuries later. He was committed to helping people find new life. His ability to come through on His promises is incredible. The thought flashed in my mind — I would love to be involved in a life like His! If He would show me the way, I would sign up. And that's what I did. I renewed my personal commitment to Christ and have been learning more about being Christlike nearly every day since.

Jesus is the greatest model for establishing and developing a relationship. Let's take a look at the kind of commitment He teaches and demonstrates. These components can transform your relationships.

**Understanding.**

Basic to any lasting relationship is empathy and understanding. There is an old Indian proverb that goes like this: "Before you criticize another brave, you must walk a mile in his moccasins." Getting into the mind and heart of another person is important. Contrary to many people's opinions, the major problem in a dating relationship is not poor communication. It is lack of understanding. You can have all the right techniques of communication, but it will be hollow if you are not committed to genuinely understanding or identifying with the other person.

A man was taking his little boy for a spring walk in flowering fields and they noticed a large ant hill. His curious son played in the dirt as the father told him about how ants build their home. After they had walked on for awhile, the man turned to look back. He saw a farmer, on his big tractor, plowing where they had seen the ant hill and realized the ants were doomed to die. In the midst of this situation he had an interesting thought. If he tried to warn the ants of the coming danger, how could he do it? They would not understand any human warning signal. Then an idea hit him: the only way to communicate effectively with ants is to become one of them.

God became human to communicate with us and to teach us about right living and relationships with both Himself and others.

How the infinite Lord became a finite man is a great mystery. I don't know how but He did. The Bible tells us, "And the Word became flesh, and dwelt among us . . ."[13]

God came out of heaven to become one of us, so He could identify with us totally — our thoughts, needs, pressures, emotions, strengths, weaknesses and temptations. "[He] has been tempted in all things as we are, yet without sin."[14] Perfect man and holy God in one — Jesus. He came to communicate God's heart and desires. Jesus wanted so much to show us His love that He sacrificed His life for us. Now that's commitment!

Put yourself into the mind and emotions of the person you are dating. This is anything but easy, especially when relating to a person of the opposite sex. Men and women think and react differently in many ways, so you have to work at understanding each other. Honestly seek to find out how your date feels about life. What would be that person's reaction to a sad movie, a dull professor, a screaming child or a traffic accident? When I got engaged, a friend of mine gave me a wise tidbit of information: "Dick, after you get married you will find out that women are wired differently." Paula and I have proved him correct hundreds of times. But we keep trying to understand. I have vowed to be a lifelong student of Paula. Class is always in session.

**Honesty.**

I have surveyed over 500 single adults and asked each one to write on a card the main reason they felt that dating couples break up. Almost 75 percent said lack of communication. You may ask, "What's wrong? Don't couples talk to each other?" Of course most do, but communication covers more than verbalization. What your partner wants to discover is not only your head, but also your heart. In every stage of a relationship there needs to be vulnerability, the freedom to express both thoughts *and* feelings.

It is here that Jesus leads the way in setting an example for us. He was transparent and honest, so much so that many people had a hard time accepting what He said. Talk about being a self-discloser! He freely expressed His emotions, both anger and compassion. He interacted with His enemies even when He knew it would eventually bring Him harm. He shared with His disciples, "I am the way, and the truth, and the life; no one comes to the Father, but through Me."[15] In saying that, He shared the very essence or core of who He was . . . the way to a relationship with God Himself! He refused to compromise the truth even when it ran against popular opinion. And He always remained steadfast in communicating God's love, mercy, forgiveness and judgment.

All of us want to be known for who we really are. Who wants to love a false image, a mask someone is wearing? Some couples play hide and seek. At times they cover up their thoughts and feelings because of fear. Other times they open little cracks in the veneer hoping the other will want to venture to investigate — but "not too much please!" We are afraid of rejection.

The apostle Paul describes what honesty is about. ". . . but speaking the truth in love, we are to grow up in all aspects into Him."[16] Truth and love are inseparable in developing and maintaining commitment.

Alan Loy McGinnis, in his popular book, *The Friendship Factor*, tells people to open up even the dark side of their lives. "I think I can even go so far as to say that you can never genuinely know yourself except as an outcome of disclosing yourself to another person; you learn how to increase contact with your real self."[17]

Cleveland McDonald emphasizes the importance of people establishing frank, open communication early in the dating relationship. "If a person is unable to talk about certain subjects to the dating partners after the relationship becomes serious, it is evident that a problem exists."[18]

Commitment opens up your heart and allows you to communicate. This is trust. But it doesn't happen all at once; it is progressive. As a dating relationship develops, self-disclosure needs to grow. For some of us, this is very difficult. But because Christ has led the way, we can do it. When we respond to His love for us, He gives us strength to be ourselves. "There is no fear in love; but perfect love casts out fear, because fear involves punishment, and the one who fears is not perfected in love. We love, because He first loved us."[19]

**Perseverence.**

Too often the attitude we have about dating is that if it doesn't go our way we will quit. We flit like a butterfly from person to person, date to date, trying to find "the perfect relationship." We seldom take time to find out who people really are. We give up too early. If you have ever seen a married person who is a flirt, you'll know this pattern can persist even after marriage.

"Commitment means to hang in there for the long haul," states McGinnis. "In any relationship, there are going to be periods when your friend is not functioning well and is not able to give generously to the friendship. The test is whether you stay and wait."[20]

Peter was one of the more outspoken of Christ's disciples. He often made statements or asked questions that no doubt embarrassed Jesus. Peter made promises he couldn't keep. And worst of all, he skipped out when Jesus needed him the most. But Jesus remained steadfast in His love toward Peter. He persevered in their relationship, even though there were many trying moments.

After Jesus arose from the dead, one of the first people He went to see was his old, fickle friend Peter. Jesus easily could have said, "You've had your chance, Buster. I'm not going to fool with you anymore." But that's not the example He set for us. He persevered in His relationship with Peter and He perseveres in His relationship with us. Over and over again, God's Word tells us how He pursues us with a never-ending love, even when we don't deserve it — nothing can ever separate us from His love.[21]

In every relationship, there will be irritation and conflicts. Chuck Swindoll has an interesting way of putting it.

> Even though you are committed . . . there will still be times of tension, tears, struggle, disagreement, and impatience. Commitment doesn't erase our humanity! That's bad news, but it's realistic. The good news is this: With the Lord Jesus Christ living within you and with His book, the Bible, waiting to be called upon for counsel and advice, no conflict is beyond solution.[22]

One thing I need to say at this point is that we have different levels of commitment. Jesus was not as committed to everyone with His time, energy and sharing as He was to that small band of twelve disciples He chose to pour His life into.

The same would be true of you. Your level of commitment to casual acquaintances would be considerably less than to those you choose to invest yourself in. With your close friends, there should be no vacillation. With the people you date, you should consciously develop aspects of understanding and compatibility so that when "the right one comes along," you will know how to be committed for a lifetime.

Jesus is our example again. In John 13:1 we read, "Jesus knowing that His hour had come that He should depart out of this world to the Father, having loved His own who were in the world, He loved them to the end."

## Giving.

We've talked about giving several times in this book so far. Earlier in this chapter, I shared how one of the reasons we find it hard to make commitments is that we are "unwilling to pay the price." Giving to others is costly.

In the chapter on self-image, I shared how one of the most effective ways to improve your self-concept is to give of yourself to others in healthy, positive ways.

Once again, Jesus provides us with the supreme example of giving. He gave His time to the sick and needy, even when He was tired. He gave food to the hungry when He fed the multitude. He gave the water of life to the woman at the well. And most of all, He gave His life so that we would no longer have to carry the heavy burden of our failures and sins — now that's commitment!

Stop and think for a moment about the people you value most in your life. Would you describe them as givers or takers? For most of us, the people we cherish are givers. They give their love to us freely; they give their time; they give us encouragement and support. Are you being that kind of person in your relationships?

I have personally found that when I feel the most unloved, that's the time I need to give the most. True sacrificial giving is not always based on how I feel; often it must be an act of my will.

Are you giving unselfishly in your relationships?

Do you truly have a giving spirit, giving to others as well as to the one you date? Do you give your time to visit the blind, elderly or sick? Do you give of your talents in your church? Do you share your personal relationship with Christ with others in need? Do you actively give love and kindness to your parents or family members? The greatest way to find love is to give love.

As we've discussed, giving to others is indeed a key principle to building lasting relationships. But there is one more key ingredient to giving that is essential for you to know.

St. Augustine had a very close friend, Nebridius, whom he loved and who gave of himself in many ways. But one day Nebridius died, and St. Augustine was crushed with grief. At the loss of his dear friend he said, "This is what comes . . . of giving one's heart to anything but God. All human beings pass away. Do not let your happiness depend on something you might lose."[23]

I have thought of that statement many times. True giving of yourself to others is essential to building lasting relationships. But every person we know will someday die. The only truly lasting relationship we can ever build is with Jesus Christ. In fact, it is through a committed relationship with Jesus Christ that we can best understand and develop a healthy relationship with another human being. Why? Because when we focus on Jesus, He helps us get rid of selfishness, anger, weakness and sin. Committing ourselves to God changes everything because He changes us, helping us to become more like Him.

Let me summarize what God wants each of us to know:

(1) Jesus Christ is the supreme example of commitment.

He is God and loves us infinitely.

(2) Because of our self-centeredness and sin, we are guilty before God. We are cut off from Him and doomed to be separated from Him — in this life and the one to come.

> For the wages of sin is death.[24] And these will pay the penalty of eternal destruction, away from the presence of the Lord and from the glory of His power.[25]

(3) Jesus Christ carried all our sin and guilt on the cross. He died for us.

> And He Himself bore our sins in His body on the cross, that we might die to sin and live to righteousness; for by His wounds you were healed.[26]

(4) When we come to the understanding of the truth and reality of Christ's death and resurrection for us, it opens the way for an intimate, eternal relationship with God. His forgiveness cleanses us from all sin, and saves us from the horror of condemnation and separation from Him.

Let me ask you a personal question. Do you now have a committed relationship with Jesus Christ? If not, would you like to establish that kind of oneness with God? It is yours when you humbly put your faith in Him. Here is God's promise. Christ said, "Truly, truly, I say to you, he who hears My Word, and believes Him who sent Me, has eternal life, and does not come into judgment, but has passed out of death into life."[27]

If you long for this special love relationship with your Creator, I invite you, right now, to put this book down and talk to Christ. Open your heart and confess your need for Him to cleanse you and give you new life — to live in you.

When you commit yourself to Him, He has promised to forgive you of your sins, enter your heart and give you strength to deal with your problems. He tells us, "Therefore if any man is in Christ, he is a new creature; the old things passed away; behold, new things have come."[28]

As I have said throughout this chapter, Christ provides us

with the best example in every area of commitment. But even more exciting, He's also concerned about every other area and need in your life. Believe Him, and let Him teach you how to relate to the opposite sex and to all of life. He wants to guide you in developing close, happy, lasting relationships. He even promises to stand by you if your relationship breaks up. We will look at that next.

# DEALING
# WITH A BREAKUP

For the book, *Singles, The New Americans*, the first major national survey was conducted with single adults (20-55) all across America. One of the questions asked was, "What is the most frequent reason you stop dating someone?" They answered as follows:

|  |  | Men | Women |
|---|---|---|---|
| A. | I find him/her dull and superficial | 30% | 34% |
| B. | (For men) She refuses to have sex | 6% | |
|  | (For women) All he wants is sex | | 13% |
| C. | He/She is immature or neurotic | 20% | 18% |
| D. | He/She is a poor lover | 3% | 3% |
| E. | It's usually my way to go out with a man/woman a few times and then move on | 15% | 8% |
| F. | (For men) She presses me too quickly for intimacy | 10% | |
|  | (For women) He shows no signs of serious interest or involvement | | 13% |
| G. | She loses interest/He stops calling | 12% | 7% |
| H. | Don't know | 5% | 6%[1] |

It's clear that there are many reasons couples break up. It has been stated that the average girl has broken at least one engagement before she marries.[2] There are no accurate statistics on how many times the typical American has terminated dating relationships, but I would guess that it would be over ten. That's a lot of hurt feelings, disappointments and painful memories. During my single years, I broke up with thirty-one different women, and five of those experiences were traumatic for me. That may or may not qualify me to write this chapter. But to be certain, I have been through the emotional wringer, and have learned some significant lessons in the process.

We've spent considerable time in this book focusing on ways to keep couples together. But there are times when breaking up is the *best* thing you can do. To leave a destructive or dead-end relationship is not necessarily the "chicken's way out." Sometimes, the most courageous thing to say is, "Our relationship is going nowhere. It is not God's best for me or for you."

As we have already seen there are several reasons couples break up. But I would like to focus on several circumstances in which you *should* break up.

## Emotional Abuse

Have you seen your dating relationship degenerate into constant arguments or little, picky criticisms? Are you being repeatedly put down in public? Does the person you are dating seem to focus often on your faults? Are there a lot of times he/she yells or swears at you or gives you disgusted looks? All these will wear you down, play upon your conscience and raise your anger level. It is terribly humiliating and degrading. No one should stand for frequent mental abuse. If you are in a dating relationship like this, the best thing to do is to get out so that you do not have severe emotional scars when your heart has been ripped apart.

### Physical Abuse

This is even more serious than emotional abuse. In a recent report in *U.S.A. Today,* there was a statement which read, "One in four teenagers has been a victim of violence on dates, and girls are as likely as boys to be violent." This was according to a study of 256 high school students in Sacramento, California. The researchers continued, "Date-beating among teenagers may be as common as wife-beating among adults." They found that 27 percent of the students surveyed reported some kind of violent behavior — slapping, punching, shoving — while on a date. "One of the sadder discoveries," said one of the researchers, "is that dating violence, in and of itself, is not enough to end a relationship."[3]

But it should be. Regardless of your age, being physically abused is degrading and destructive. It also can be a sign that your dating partner is tremendously immature, or possibly even emotionally unbalanced, needing the attention of a counselor.

There are natural differences in every relationship of course which allow for healthy arguments and disagreements. But if the person you are dating hits, pinches, shoves, slaps or throws things at you in a fit of anger, then you should say goodbye. Is there ever a good excuse for intentionally causing physical pain or harm? No.

### Spiritual Mismatch

When I was a pastor, there were a number of women who came to my church whose husbands would never come. They were men who had no desire for anything spiritual. Realize that when you become emotionally involved with a non-Christian, your perspective is clouded and it is very difficult to say no to that relationship. No matter how special, that person cannot give you a deeper spiritual perspective. According to 1 Corinthians, the person without Jesus Christ "does not accept the things of the Spirit of God; they are foolishness to him, and he cannot understand them,"[4] so you are on two completely different wavelengths.

If you genuinely want to follow Christ and let Him be your guide, but you are dating a non-Christian, then you are setting yourself up for pain and misery. The Bible clearly says in 2 Corinthians that we should "not be bound together with unbelievers; for what partnership have righteousness and lawlessness, or what fellowship has light with darkness?"[5] Non-Christians are self-reliant, depending upon their own knowledge rather than upon God for answers and direction. Their principles of living are built upon their own perception, not upon God's. They may even try to fool you by going to church, hoping that will somehow persuade you of their interest. However, I would be very cautious of their motives.

A true Christian can be known by the fruits of his life: "love, joy, peace, patience, kindness, goodness, faithfulness, gentleness, self-control."[6]

I have seen it happen many times: A guy goes to church with his girlfriend because he knows she is a Christian. He likes her and is determined that she love him. But once they get married, he no longer shows interest in a spiritual life. He had never honestly humbled himself before God. Each partner actually inhabits a different world. And now she is trapped. I wish I could say this has happened only a very few times. But I could find you thousands of men and women who are less than fulfilled today because they are not united in spirit with their mates.

If you are willing to accept a less-than-best (and often times miserable) relationship, then dating someone of "a different world" is a quick way to get there. However, I strongly encourage you *not* to accept less than God's very best for your life.

Before I continue, let me assure you that I am not saying

you should never associate with non-Christians. In fact I would say just the opposite. Christians are the light of the world and the salt of the earth. One of the primary ways non-Christians have a chance to see and experience Christ's love is through relating with Christians. However we do need to see the definite difference between associating with non-Christians and dating them. Feelings and emotions have such a powerful influence in dating relationships that they often cause us to lose perspective and balance.

So yes, by all means, develop non-Christian friendships. But confine your primary dating relationships to those who are of like mind and spirit. Be aware that dating a non-Christian is a dead-end street.

Another situation to be cautious of is a worldly Christian. This is someone who has made a personal decision for Christ, but is not walking in a warm, tender, consistent way with the Lord. This individual knows the Christian jargon, but exhibits no vital spiritual life. He may go to church, but sooner or later you can discern that there is no humble attitude toward God. The opinions and ways of the world have become too important to him. There is no seeking of the Lord and little interest in obeying God's word by living a righteous life.

Even if you are deeply committed to following Christ, your partner can dampen your spirit, drag you down and cause you to compromise your commitment and feelings about the Lord. Maybe you want to live for God and share your faith with other people, but your partner belittles you for doing so. A worldly Christian can easily throw water on one who is enthusiastic about Christ. He can neutralize you and cause you to lose the kind of witness that you had.

If you are dating either a non-Christian or a worldly Christian, I would strongly urge you to think about the implications of being unequally yoked. Wait for someone that your spirit can become united with, so together you can encourage each other to seek Christ faithfully in all situations and circumstances.

There is no greater joy than to have that common oneness in a relationship. When problems come, you can go with each other to the Lord and seek His guidance and understanding. When you have perplexities and bewilderment, you can find His answers in the Bible. He has promised always to lead and guide us.[7] You can know He will mold your hearts into one. That kind of joy and intimacy with Christ and with each other is the only kind that will deeply satisfy your heart.

The above three reasons I personally consider to be the most clear-cut reasons to redefine and/or make major changes in your relationships. However, there are several other significant signs to watch for.

### Different Life Goals

Some difference in perspective is good. In fact, often it is these differences which attract us to each other. However, when two people have different values and are going in different directions, and when their goals do not complement each other, it may be an indication that they are not compatible. Some imperative questions are, what do you want to do with your life? What motivates you? What causes you to have a sense of direction and purpose? Is that purpose compatible with the purpose of the person you are dating?

George wanted to be a traveling salesman, to travel all over the western states, but Beth, whom he was dating, wanted to study for a doctorate and believed very strongly in settling down and developing well-established roots. They had very different goals in life and neither wanted to change. Another fellow, Steve, felt that God was calling him to the mission field to spend his life helping people in the rural areas of an Asian country, but Pam, his fiancé, wanted to be a high school teacher in a large city in America. Both couples tried for a very long time to develop compatibility, but their divergent purposes eventually caused them to break their engagements.

Many times we will set aside our purposes for the other individual. Some of this is good because it helps mold us into one, but there can also be strong innate motivating factors which can drive us worlds apart. It is very important to discuss and understand each other's purposes and goals and to help each other reach those goals, even if it means not being a couple.

## No Joy

Has the relationship become a drudgery? There will be times in any relationship when either one or the other person feels down or dejected. However, when this lack of enthusiasm continues for a long period, then it is time to evaluate your relationship. Is the fun gone? Do you sense you are moving toward a real future or are you just hanging on because you enjoy the security? When you think about spending the rest of your life with this person, do you still get excited? You will be spending thousands of hours alone, just the two of you. You'd better enjoy it. Are you taking this person for granted? Have you stopped encouraging each other to develop and expand your horizons? Now is the time to take a close look at your compatibility and your prospects for a future together. If consistent boredom has set in, then a re-evaluation of your relationship is in order.

## Smothered Self-Expression

Do your personality, attitudes and actions please your date? Does your partner want you to act a certain way or wear certain clothes which are *not* "you"? Have you been pressured to change your friends? Or even yourself? Or are you, maybe, doing these things to your partner? We all have something inside of us that screams out to be loved for who we are and not for what the other person wants to make of us. Can you both openly share your fears, loneliness, dreams and sorrows or do you have to wear a mask and put on a front? If you are in a relationship in which either individual does not love the other for who that person is, then you are going to find painful conflicts recurring over and over. This is another good reason to terminate your relationship.

## Overemphasis On Sex

We've already spent an entire chapter on sexual burnout, so we will only mention it here briefly. It is another reason to consider breaking up.

If you totally took away the physical part of your relationship for one or two months, would your partner still want to date you? Does your partner allow and encourage all aspects of the relationship to grow rather than letting the physical part become overpowering? When you say no to being involved sexually, does your partner respect and support you? Do you find it easier to make-out than to talk?

Sex is wonderful when it is enjoyed as God intended. It is a beautiful part of the intimate marriage relationship. But when it is not kept in its proper place, it can become a consuming lust that can make each of you insensitive to the real needs and feelings of the other.

## Lack Of Trust

Does your partner usually make you feel boxed in or smothered with attention? Do you constantly receive phone calls to see where you have been, what you have been doing and all the other little details of life? Do one or both of you constantly assume negative intent on the part of each other?[8] This lack of trust can cause you to feel stress and pressure. It inhibits the freedom to expand your horizons and to grow. It makes you want to escape. No one wants to feel under someone else's control. It is unfortunate that many good relationships with great potential have developed insecurities and mistrust. Neither partner is then able to be free. Lack of trust kills relationships.

## HOW TO BREAK UP

In each of the eight circumstances mentioned above, there are ways you could find to overcome and remedy the situation. In fact, I encourage you to find a remedy if at all possible. This book is about building lasting relationships, remember? However, if these problems continue for a period of time and you find yourself simply "going through the motions" with little or no cooperation from your partner, it is time to reconsider the relationship or at least redefine it. If it is not a relationship that builds either you or your partner then the hard decision of breaking up must be made.

No, it is not usually an easy thing to do. When you break up there probably will be some pain. In some ways it's like taking off a bandage. When I was a little boy and wanted to take a bandage off, I would do it very, very slowly so I wouldn't pull any hair. It would take me a good 20 minutes to work the bandage loose slowly and even then it hurt a little. But I did everything I could to minimize the pain. My mother took another approach. She would see me babying the bandage and she'd say, "Oh, you want to get it off?" Then she'd just rip it off. Man, did it hurt! But the pain was then quickly over. When you break up there's going to be pain — either way you do it, slow or fast. That's why breaking up usually requires tremendous courage and honesty. But when done in genuine love, it can be one of the best things for both of you.

Here are six steps to follow that will help you say goodbye.

(1) *Seek God's wisdom and guidance.* In James 1:2-8, we

read that God will give you wisdom in what to do and how to do it. When going through the difficult and painful task of severing a relationship, it's great to know God's hand is guiding you. He promises to go before you and give you courage and strength.

In the struggle of trying to determine His will, I have often turned to Proverbs 3:5-6. "Trust in the Lord with *all* your heart, and do not lean on your own understanding. In *all* your ways acknowledge Him, and He will make your paths straight." The Lord is interested in everything about you and desires to show you the steps to take so that your decisions and actions will be the best for you and for others.

God not only gives you guidance, but also strength to do what is right. The apostle Paul expressed his thanks to God for His power to do the impossible: "Now to Him who is able to do exceeding abundantly beyond all that we ask or think, according to the power that works within us, to Him be the glory in the church and in Christ Jesus to *all* generations forever and ever."[9] His power works to overcome our weakness and fear. Saying goodbye to someone you have been dating is not easy. Emotions and nervousness can make the situation tense and awkward. God's courage and guidance are available to you when you trust Him.[10]

Seek His wisdom. Ask Him for help. He understands what you are feeling and the difficult place in which you find yourself. And remember, He definitely wants you to know the happiness and joy of a relationship that builds you up and fulfills you, instead of one that tears you down and fragments you.

He is the God of all peace and comfort. You can always come to Him knowing He is there to help you. Trust Him. He knows what is best for you, and He wants to help you find it.

(2) *Prepare yourself.* Think through as clearly as possible your reasons and motives for breaking up. What are the contributing factors that have brought you to this decision? Are your

motives honest, kind and clear? Are they consistent with God's Word?

Never break up merely to get attention or sympathy or to elicit a deeper commitment from your partner. That is playing a deceitful game. Never break up just to express anger or hostility or to "put someone in his place." Although strong emotions may be involved, express your thoughts decisively and firmly — but kindly.

If the other person does not want to break up, you may be confronted with defensive feelings and attempts to hold on to the relationship. When you clearly understand the things that are causing you to break up, and when you express them honestly, clearly and calmly, you will be able to handle the pleas from the other person more effectively. Have your conclusions and reasons well thought out ahead of time. (Writing them down can be very helpful.)

(3) *Ask close friends for advice.* Go to some strong Christians you know and can trust. Your pastor or an older couple may be able to help you. Share with them your situation. In sharing, do not spread lies or half-truths to gain support for your side. Simply tell them your honest thoughts and feelings. Ask for their advice and prayer support. What would they do in your situation? Do they agree with your approach? Can they support you in your action? Proverbs says, "The way of a fool is right in his own eyes, but a wise man is he who listens to counsel."[11]

(4) *Get together.* If at all possible, find a time and a place where you and your dating partner can meet alone. Never try to break up in public or in front of friends. That would be very embarrassing for both of you and could easily cause resentment. If you are geographically separated, if the situation is too threatening or if you are afraid of physical abuse, write to the person. There are lots of jokes about "Dear John letters," but in reality, you often can express your feelings more clearly in a letter. It

can be a very practical and mature way of ending a relationship. Follow up with a phone call to make sure you were understood and talk it over with a positive attitude. If possible however, it is preferable to meet face to face. Since you have shared your life in a special way, it is a gracious thing to close the relationship in a personal conversation together. When you look for a place, choose a non-romantic setting. It is much easier to weaken or back down on your intentions in this emotional time, but later you would regret it.

Remember to allow time for talking and sharing feelings. Don't just drop the bomb and leave. Discuss the situation. Endeavor not to be hurried or just to blurt out your decision without being sensitive to the other person's reactions. Be firm, but treat the person as you would want to be treated in the same situation.

(5) *Tell the truth in love.* Ephesians says, "But speaking the truth in love, we are to grow up in all aspects into Him, who is the head, even Christ."[12] To speak the truth in love means that truth without love is harsh, just as love without truth is hollow. We need both truthful love and loving truth. Do not play games. It is easy to make double-meaning statements and tell half-truths or "little white lies." But be honest; try to express your reasons and your feelings as tactfully and positively as possible. It may be very difficult with your emotions so involved, but you can rely upon Christ to give you wisdom and peace of mind. Express very openly that you appreciate and value your friendship; however, you do not desire your relationship to continue on a romantic basis. And if you feel it would be best not to see the person for awhile because of deep hurt or a potentially uncomfortable situation, be open with your feelings and expectations. Tell the truth, but do it in love.

If the individual has bad habits or attitudes that are definitely wrong, express these in a gentle but positive manner. The book of Matthew in the New Testament tells us we are to confront a person who has sinned and done something wrong.[13] It is important to help the person realize that although your relationship is no longer the same, you want to build him up. Do not act like a boss or a judge or make personal attacks. Rather, point out in love the things that concern you. Do not hurt the other person on purpose even if you have been hurt yourself. The way you say things can mean the difference between devastation and development.

On the other hand, is it possible that you are the one who has not acted properly at times? Have you wrongfully hurt your dating partner? If so, you need to seek forgiveness for your unloving actions or attitudes. We should seek forgiveness and cleansing first from God. If we humbly come to Him with our sins and disobedience, He removes all barriers that prevent us from having close fellowship with Him.[14]

However, Christ has added a new dimension. "If therefore you are presenting your offering (gifts) at the altar, and there remember that your brother has something against you, leave your offering there before the altar, and go your way; first be reconciled to your brother, and then come and present your offering."[15] It is a wonderful thing to have a clear conscience before God and before a person you have wronged. Take that difficult step of forgiveness. Even if the person is obstinate and refuses to forgive you because of the pain he feels, you can walk away free. You have taken the proper approach. Your acceptance is in God. He has cleansed you and does not condemn.[16] The memory of your behavior may linger, but you have received God's forgiveness. Learn from the experience so that in a future relationship you will act differently.

When I was dating a girl named Gail, I did several very selfish things. I did not show deep concern for the problems she faced with her parents and in school. My lack of thoughtfulness bothered her. She became frustrated with me and eventually broke off our relationship. I was blind to my self-centeredness. Several weeks later I finally realized I had acted selfishly and asked her to forgive me. Although we never had another date, my conscience was cleared. Through it all, God taught me some significant lessons, and I learned to be more sensitive and kind to the women I dated.

My wife and I have been very thankful for past relationships because we learned things from them, things which have helped develop our present attitudes and behavior. Therefore, when we came together, each benefited from many of the painful lessons we had learned in the past.

(6) *Be definite.* The person may try to dissuade you or may become angry and defensive. Your emotions may be in an upheaval. However, the Bible says to "let your yes be yes, and your no, no."[17] If you vacillate, the person may take advantage of your indecisiveness and may try to play on your emotions to make you feel guilty or unsure. However, if you have thought through your reasons clearly and have sensed God's guidance, then in a gentle and kind manner, you can be clear and firm.

There is a place, however, for reconsideration. If the things that really bother you are discussed openly and sincere steps are planned to change unwanted behavior, you might choose to continue the relationship. But if in your heart and mind you believe you definitely should not continue, then you should express that. Make a clean break. Sever the relationship, but do not destroy the person in the process. Give time for a response, but stick to your guns. Remember, it is important to realize you can love a person without wanting to be married to that person. Not all love is marriage love.

## AFTER THE BREAKUP

Just as there is a healing process that must take place after surgery, there are several things that need to take place in your life after you break up (or after someone else breaks up with you).

(1) *Feel your feelings:* It is okay to express grief, pain and hurt. These things often well up within us. If we put a lid on them and try to smother them, eventually they will return in a more destructive manner. Our bodies will take the toll of these emotions if we do not allow them to be expressed. Don't be phony, exuding friendliness and smiles, when deep down inside you are ready to explode. None of us likes rejection, so don't be ashamed or embarrassed about expressing your hurt. If you are sad, it's okay to cry.

My wife Paula told me about a time she broke up with a fellow she liked very much. She felt so down that she decided to go to a sad movie. The movie made her cry even more. But in expressing her grief and letting it out, healing began because she was able to reach down inside her heart and understand what she was going through.

If you are rejected by one person, it does not mean the next person will reject you. And of course, it does not mean that you are some sort of reject yourself. You were made for healthy, happy relationships.

(2) *Find comfort in the Lord.* He is the one who is always there, even when you feel lonely and depressed; even when it seems like the world is coming to an end. God has not left you. He has said in the book of Jeremiah, "I have loved you with an everlasting love; therefore I have drawn you with loving kindness."[18] That love is constant and consistent even in your pain.

Remember Amy in chapter one? When she broke up with me at the beginning of my senior year in college, I was an emotional basket-case. I was so angry and upset that I began to hate her for all the pain and confusion she had caused me.

One day I was sitting in the school library trying to study. My mind was filled with self-pity and my heart was filled with hatred. But, in my hostility, Christ began to remind me of Scriptures I had read years previously.

*Dick,* God said in my mind, *I want you to love her.*

*Love her?* I thought. *Impossible! How could You ask me to love her after what she has done to me?*

It was the first time in my life I could not control my mind. I hated her even though I knew I was wrong. But I felt overwhelmed by my emotions.

Then the Lord reminded me of a passage in 2 Corinthians. Paul had a "thorn in the flesh." Some scholars think Paul had an incurable, painful eye disease. Others believe he was plagued with epilepsy or personal problems. Whatever the problem was, it was excruciatingly difficult for him. He could not handle it. So, he begged God three times that it might depart from him.

> And He has said to me, "My grace is sufficient for you, for power is perfected in weakness." Most gladly, therefore, I will rather boast about my weaknesses, that the power of Christ may dwell in me. Therefore I am well content with weaknesses, with insults, with distresses, with persecutions, with difficulties, [with break ups], for Christ's sake; For when I am weak, then I am strong.[19]

In my time of helplessness and weakness, Christ promised to give me His comfort and strength. Because Christ is in my life, I can find a way through my deepest problems.

I memorized and meditated on those verses. "When I am weak, then I am strong [in His power]." Even though the tension, pain and hurt lasted for months, Christ gradually took away the bitterness and hostility. Every time I was tempted to indulge in self-pity and anger, those verses popped into my mind. I clung to Christ, and His strength overshadowed my weaknesses. Gradually, He brought love into my heart for Amy.

Not marriage love, but a kindness and genuine desire to keep her as a friend. My life was not shattered. God was in control! He would lead me to the woman of His choice and in His time. I was secure in His eternal acceptance of me!

Saturate your mind with God's Word. And let it permeate the very fibers of your being. Meditate upon God's promises. They will help you overcome and see life more positively. Express your troubles and your heart to Him. "Let it all hang out" before the Lord. But remember also to thank Him for His goodness and power, even through your tears. "But they who seek the Lord shall not be in want of any good thing."[20]

(3) *Recognize the lessons.* What can you learn from this experience? What are some qualities you most appreciated in this person? Are there negative qualities in your life that you would like to avoid in future relationships? Based on this experience, how can you change your habit patterns to make future relationships better? Many people go from relationship to relationship and remain blind to certain problems in their lives.

I have a neighbor with whom I have jogged many times. It was a shock to find, when I came home recently from a speaking tour, that his wife had kicked him out of the house and filed for divorce. It was the second marriage for both of them. As I reflected on past conversations with them, I realized that they had not learned lessons from their previous relationships, and now their four children are faced with another broken marriage.

Take a close look at those things which you do not like about yourself and endeavor to make the necessary changes. If you take the specific steps to re-program habit patterns where change is needed, you will improve and develop your life. But don't be too hard on yourself because all of life is a growing process.

God has assured us that we are fully accepted by Him due to our relationship with Christ.[21] So we have the security of being in God's hands and the joy of knowing the Lord is developing us into mature people.[22]

(4) *Remain firm in your decision.* Although there may be room for reconciliation, many times this is not wise. It is very easy in moments of weakness or loneliness to go back to that relationship, even if your reasons for breaking up were very clear and definite. We may remember just the positive, good, fun times together and overlook the negatives, trying to find an excuse to go back to the person. However, remain true to the things that you have decided and prayed about. You cannot continue to see the person after the breakup and do the same old things together. It will be a lot harder on you to bring up painful memories, listen to old favorite records, keep special photos with you, go to favorite restaurants and places that you frequented together. It is like digging up a dead dog. It can be very unpleasant. To try to keep the relationship in your mind will only bring further pain and prolong the agony. Break away. Move into the future.

Breaking away is easier to do if you are the one who initiated the decision to terminate the dating relationship. However, when you are on the receiving end of a breakup, you will probably experience more hurt. As you seek God's strength to handle the difficult situation, take the appropriate steps to clear your mind of the relationship.

Both of you need room to heal. Some distance is very good. The old saying that time heals all wounds is very true. But it is also true that distance helps.

(5) *Forge ahead.* For awhile you may have the tendency to compare new dating partners with the one you broke up with. Remember, however, that each person is unique. Give a new relationship an opportunity to grow. And never stop reaching out to others. In your hurt and your pain, do not withdraw, but open your heart. Share the things you've learned and when

opportunity arises, date other people. You may not be romanti-cally inclined, but enjoy relating as friends. Get to know people of the opposite sex, even those you feel you would probably never marry. They are individuals with whom you can learn to develop good friendships. Believe in yourself and consciously develop your self-confidence. Remember that God is not through with you yet.

Even if every person in the world were to reject you, the Lord never will. In fact, you can endure the pain of rejection and broken dreams easier because He determines your value, not any human being. When you trust your life to Jesus, you will never lose. According to Mark 8:34, you are worth the whole world, so understand that you can have a good view of yourself because God is upholding you, developing you, giving you per-spective. Forge ahead, reach out and give yourself to other people in healthy, growing relationships.

# MELTING THE WALL OF ICE

## Epilogue

It was a gorgeous, clear morning in the Colorado Rocky Mountains. The rushing stream cascaded over huge boulders and birds sang in the aspen trees. It was a delightful scene.

But I was miserable! Glen and I had pitched our tent next to that stream the previous night so we could be far from the tent where our dates slept. Things just were not going too well, especially between me and my date.

We had come up to the mountains during a break. I had just finished teaching at the Institute of Biblical Studies held each summer at Colorado State University. So, before the next sessions, the four of us, along with a carload of others, had headed for the beautiful mountains.

Although we had known each other for a year, we had been dating for only about a month. But on this short trip, our relationship started to deteriorate.

Have you ever sensed that a wall of ice was forming between you and your date? Everything you say is taken wrong. Conversation is strained and the heart is cold. No matter what you try to do, it goes over like a lead balloon. Eventually, you just give up trying. You dread the time spent together so you end up looking at your watch hoping for the end to come soon. That's the way I felt.

I don't usually pick up hints very well, but I was getting her message loud and clear. Her shoulder was colder than the snow on the mountaintops. Oh, we talked, but it was to fill up the silence rather than to share the breathtaking beauty we saw all around us.

One evening we had fun — Joan, Glen and me. We had pitched our tents and the three of us stretched out on the blanket looking up at the stars. They were so clear that you could almost reach up and touch one. My date sat alone over by the fire even though it wasn't cold. What a boring time for her — and for me.

Three long days of this ice wall. I was miserable. When I woke up the last morning of our trip, I decided to go downstream. Sitting on a large rock in the stream bed, I thought about our relationship. As far as I was concerned, it was finished. I was writing her off my list. The pain of rejection was too much to bear. I had had it!

I had carried a small New Testament with me and I chose a passage from Luke 6 to read. I needed something to get my mind off the situation.

"But I say to you who hear," Jesus proclaimed, "love your enemies."[1] To me it was obvious: He was talking about my date. Look at what she had done to me! Pain.

"Do good to those who hate you." Jesus really understood my date and her attitude toward me.

"Bless those who curse you," He went on. "Pray for those who mistreat you."[2] My date sure had mistreated me.

My attention, as I read the rest of the passage, was on my pain and hurt. Since I had felt rejected, I was going to reject her!

But then I came to the eye opener — Luke 6:38.

"Give and it will be given to you," Jesus promised. "For whatever measure you deal out to others, it will be dealt to you in return."

I was startled! My focus had been on myself and not on her needs. I had only wanted out of the relationship. I was hurt and I wanted to hurt back.

Christ's emphasis was on love — *my* attention was on

"your enemies." His command, to "do good" — I saw only "those who hate you." I did not want to give to her, I wanted to reject her.

My self-centeredness and sin became hideous to me. I could not fathom how rotten my attitude had become. I had allowed myself to wallow in self-pity and pain.

Christ, said, "Love." How? I am weak and hurt. She deserves to be rejected and hurt in return. But Jesus had given Himself on the cross for people who were a lot worse than she was. He loved His enemies. Could I give to my date?

My heart broke and I sobbed, "Oh Lord, I need You! Change my hardness and forgive my selfishness. Fill me with Your love and power."

I was scared, but now I wanted to give to my date. The ice wall had to be melted — even if we never went out again.

The camp was empty. Over an hour had elapsed since my departure. I looked all over for her. Way up stream she was sitting with her back toward me, on some boulders. She did not notice me as I approached her. My legs felt like rubber. All courage left me and I wanted to hide. "Give, and it will be given to you" kept filling my mind. I called on Jesus for strength and wisdom to know what to say.

"Hi, mind if I join you for a few minutes?" I timidly asked.

"No, I don't mind," she replied with a surprised look on her face.

"What are you doing?" I felt like I had just swallowed my tongue.

"Oh, just thinking and reading. What have you been doing?"

"Oh, reading. Can I show what I read?" My heart was pounding.

"Sure."

I fumbled through the pages. "Love your enemies." I did

not add, "that means you."

I read the whole passage and finally got to "Give, and it will be given to you." I stopped and looked up at her. The moment had come! But I knew that somehow Christ would help me through this torture.

"Uh . . . these last four days have been difficult ones for me. There is something wrong with our relationship. I have tried to be friendly and help you have a good time, but things have not worked out very well between us." I paused and got my breath. This is the hardest conversation I have had in years, I thought.

"I had decided to not date you anymore. When I read this passage this morning, God opened my mind toward you. With all honesty, I want to give to you. I really like you. However, your desire may be to stop dating me. That's okay. I just want to let you know, my heart is open to build our friendship. I don't want any walls or any bad feelings between us."

She looked down at the rocks and slowly asked, "Would you like me to tell you what has been on my mind?"

"Yes! I would like to know."

"Well, I started to like you," she blurted out. "But to protect myself from possibly getting hurt, I became overly critical of you. That's why I acted so distant. I did not know how to handle my feelings."

I was speechless! In my wildest imagination I never guessed that would be her response. As we talked further about the situation and cleared up the misconceptions, joy and excitement flooded my heart.

I gave her a big hug and said, "It is so much better to be vulnerable and honest. The Lord Jesus gets the credit for breaking down the wall between us. Would you like to thank Him with me for this guidance?"

"I would love to."

#### CHAPTER NINE

There on the rocks we poured out our hearts to God in thanksgiving and joy.

Seven months later I was speaking at a large meeting at West Virginia University. During my talk on "How to Know When You Are in Love," I used this incident in Colorado as an illustration of giving in a relationship.

At the end of the meeting, we had an open forum time.

After several questions were asked, one student spoke up, "What ever happened to that girl you were on the rocks with?"

"What day is it today?" I asked.

"It's Thursday, January 28," somebody else replied.

"Well, in two days I plan to ask her to marry me!"

The whole auditorium erupted in cheers and applause.

Two days later, in a quiet romantic restaurant in Atlanta, I asked. Paula was speechless. She had not expected it. The next day, she said, "Yes!"

On May 30, 1982, we exchanged rings during our wedding ceremony. Inscribed on the inside of each ring is Luke 6:38: "Give and it shall be given to you!"

# NOTES

## CHAPTER 1—THERE IS HOPE

1. Jeannye Thornton, "Behind a Surge in Suicides of Young People," *U.S. News and World Report* (June 20, 1983), p. 66.

## CHAPTER 2—REMOVING THE MASKS

1. Howard Markman, "Prediction of Marital Distress," *Journal of Consulting and Clinical Psychology* (October 1981), p. 760.
2. Jess Lair, "Finding the Spot That's Right for You," *New Woman* (July 1982), p. 74.
3. David Smith, *The Friendless American Male,* Ventura, CA: Regal Books (1983), p. 22.
4. J. Grant Howard, *The Trauma of Transparency,* Portland, OR: Multnomah Press (1979), pp. 26-27.
5. Harry Zehner, "50 Shrinks Give Their Rx for Marital Happiness," *Cosmopolitan* (June 1982), p. 223.
6. C. S. Lewis, *The Four Loves,* New York: Harcourt Brace Jovanovich, Inc. (1960), p. 169.
7. Zehner, "50 Shrinks," p. 223.

## CHAPTER 3—HANDLING UNREALISTIC EXPECTATIONS

1. Harry Zehner, "50 Shrinks Give Their Rx for Marital Happiness," *Cosmopolitan* (June 1982), p. 220.
2. Norman Wright and Marvin Inman, *A Guidebook to Dating, Waiting and Choosing a Mate,* Eugene, OR: Harvest House Publishers (1978), p. 149.
3. Jacqueline Simenauer and David Carroll, *Singles — The New Americans,* New York: New American Library (1982), p. 120.
4. Zehner, "50 Shrinks," p. 272.
5. Zehner, "50 Shrinks," p. 222.
6. Frederic Flach, "What Effect Does the Entertainment Industry Have on Sexual Attitudes and Behavior?" *Medical Aspects of Human Sexuality* (November 1982), p. 34DD.
7. "Janet Dailey, Queen of Hearts," *Redbook* (June 1983), p. 66.
8. Zehner, "50 Shrinks," p. 223.
9. Corrie Ten Boom, *Corrie Ten Boom: Clippings From My Notebook,* Nashville, TN: Thomas Nelson, Inc. (1982), p. 51.
10. I. Phillips Frohman, "Unrealistic Expectations of Marriage," *Medical Aspects of Human Sexuality* (October 1981), p. 51.
11. Alan Loy McGinnis, *The Romance Factor,* New York: Harper and Row (1982), p. 75.

## CHAPTER 4—LIKING YOURSELF SO OTHERS CAN TOO

1. Song of Solomon 1:5-7.
2. James Dobson, *Hide or Seek,* Old Tappan, NJ: Fleming H. Revell Co. (1974), p. 136.
3. Holman Cooper and Braithwaite, "Self-Esteem and Family Cohesion; The Child's Perspective and Adjustment," *The Journal of Marriage and the Family* (February 1983), p. 153.
4. Matthew 11:28.
5. Stanley Coppersmith, *The Antecedents of Self-Esteem,* San Francisco: W. H. Freeman and Company (1967), p. 3.
6. Nathaniel Branden, *The Psychology of Self-Esteem — A NEW Concept of Man's Psychological Nature,* Los Angeles: Nash Publishing Corporation (1969), p. 231.
7. Eugene Mathes and Nancy Severa, "Jealousy, Romantic Love, and Liking," *Psychological Reports* 49 (August 1981), p. 26.
8. Mathes and Severa, "Jealousy . . ." p. 26.
9. Kenneth Gergen, *The Concept of Self,* San Francisco: Holt, Rinehart and Winston, Inc. (1971), p. 67.
10. Joseph Aldrich, *Self Worth — How to Become More Loveable,* Portland, OR: Multnomah Press (1982), p. 11.
11. Larry Bailey, "Focus of Fulfillment," *Journal of Psychology and Theology* 4:3 (Fall 1975), p. 296.
12. 2 Corinthians 5:14, 15.
13. Hebrews 13:5.

## CHAPTER 5—ABOLISHING THE 50/50 APPROACH

1. See Phillips Frohman, "Unrealistic Expectations of Marriage," *Medical Aspects of Human Sexuality* (October 1981), p. 54.
2. Don Meredith, *Becoming One,* Nashville: Thomas Nelson, Inc. (1979), p. 38.
3. Stan Albrecht and Phillip Kunz, *Journal of Divorce* 3 (Summer 1980), p. 324.
4. Daniel Yankelovich, *New Rules,* New York: Bantam Books (1981), p. 248.
5. Ezekiel 36:26.
6. Ezekiel 36:27.
7. Matthew 6:32, 33.
8. James Lynch, "Warning: Living Alone Is Dangerous to Your Health," *U.S. News and World Report* (June 30, 1980), p. 48.
9. Larry Bailey, "Focus of Fulfillment," *Journal of Psychology and Theology* 4:3 (Fall 1975), p. 296.
10. Acts 20:35.

## CHAPTER 6—ENJOYING SEXUAL SANITY

1. Peter Marin, "The Broken Promises of the Sex Revolution," *Psychology Today* (July 1983), p. 53.

2.  Norman Wright and Marvin Inmon, *A Guidebook to Dating, Waiting and Choosing a Mate,* Eugene, OR: Harvest House Publishers (1978), pp. 145-146.

3.  Cherie Burns, "What No One Ever Told Us About Sexual Freedom," *Glamour* (August 1982), p. 260.

4.  Gabrielle Brown, *The New Celibacy,* New York: McGraw-Hill Book Company (1980), p. 76.

5.  See Jacqueline Simenauer and David Carroll, *Singles — The New Americans,* New York: New American Library (1982), p. 366.

6.  C. Stephen Board, *His Guide to Sex, Singleness and Marriage,* Downers Grove, IL: Inter-Varsity Press (1974), p. 17.

7.  Alexander Astin, "Freshman Characteristics and Attitudes," *The Chronicle of Higher Education* (January 26, 1983), p. 12.

8.  Howard and Martha Lewis, "How to Talk With Teen-Agers About Virginity," *Families* (November 1981), p. 69.

9.  Lewis, ". . . Virginity," p. 74.

10. Simenauer and Carroll, *Singles,* p. 165.

11. Sinemauer and Carroll, *Singles,* p. 160.

12. James Dobson, *Emotions — Can You Trust Them?* Ventura, CA: Gospel Light Publications (1980), p. 57.

13. Elizabeth Hall, "A Conversation With Erik Erikson," *Psychology Today* (June 1983), p. 25.

14. C. Roy Fowler, "Disillusionment With 'Sexual Freedom,' " *Medical Aspects of Human Sexuality* (July 1983), p. 13.

15. Quoted by Gabrielle Brown in *The New Celibacy,* p. 61.

16. Brown, *New Celibacy,* p. 61.

17. See Romans 2:15.

18. John 8:34.

19. Genesis 2:24.

20. See Deuteronomy 30:20. Cleave is translated as "holding fast."

21. Josh McDowell and Paul Lewis, *Givers, Takers and Other Kinds of Lovers,* Chicago: Tyndale House Publishers (1980), p. 30.

22. Luke 12:2,3.

23. I Thessalonians 4:3-8.

24. I John 1:9.

25. John White, *Eros Defiled,* Downers Grove, IL: Inter-Varsity Press (1977), p. 51.

## CHAPTER 7—COMMITMENT: THE FORGOTTEN KEY

1.  Erich Fromm, *The Art of Loving,* New York: Bantam Books (1963), p. 107.

2.  See Daniel Yankelovich, *New Rules,* New York: Bantam Books (1981), p. 96.

3.  "Marriage — It's Back In Style," *U.S. News and World Report* (June 20, 1983), p. 46.

4.  See Jacqueline Simenauer and David Carroll, *Singles — The New Americans,* New York: New American Library (1982), p. 267.

5. "Ava Just Wanted To Be a Homebody," *San Bernardino* (California) *Sun* (December 14, 1982), p. C-1.

6. C. S. Lewis, *The Four Loves,* New York: Harcourt Brace Jovanovich, Inc. (1960), p. 169.

7. Daniel Goleman, "Make-Or-Break Resolutions," *Psychology Today* (January 1982), p. 20.

8. Jerry Jones, "A Conversation With Tony Campolo," *Solo, The Christian Magazine for Single Adults* (March 1983), p. 32.

9. John Powell, *Why Am I Afraid to Tell You Who I Am?* Hiles, IL: Argus Communications (1969(, p. 134.

10. Yankelovich, *New Rules,* p. 145.

11. See Jerry Jones, "A Conversation With Andre Bustanoby," *Solo, The Christian Magazine for Single Adults* (Fall 1983), p. 23.

12. See Yankelovich, *New Rules,* p. 248.

13. John 1:14.

14. Hebrews 4:15.

15. John 14:6.

16. Ephesians 4:15.

17. Alan Loy McGinnis, *The Friendship Factor,* Minneapolis, MN: Augsburg Publishing House (1979), p. 34.

18. Cleveland McDonald, *Creating a Successful Christian Marriage,* Grand Rapids, MI: Baker Book House (1981), p. 52.

19. 1 John 4:18,19.

20. McGinnis, *Friendship Factor,* p. 176.

21. Romans 8:32-39.

22. Charles Swindoll, *Commitment,* Portland, OR: Multnomah Press (1981), p. 15.

23. Lewis, *Four Loves,* p. 167.

24. Romans 6:23.

25. 2 Thessalonians 1:9.

26. 1 Peter 2:24.

27. John 5:24.

28. 2 Corinthians 5:17.

## CHAPTER 8—DEALING WITH A BREAKUP

1. Jacqueline Simenauer and David Carroll, *Singles — The New Americans,* New York: New American Library (1982), pp. 120-121.

2. See Paul Barkman, "Breaking Up," *Campus Life* (May '1974), p. 75.

3. "Date Beating: It's Fairly Common for Teens," *USA Today* (June 16, 1983), p. 3D.

4. 1 Corinthians 2:14.

5. 2 Corinthians 6:14.

6. Galatians 5:22,23.

7. See Romans 12:1,2.

8. Carmen Lynch and Blinder, "The Romantic Relationship," *Medical Aspects of Human Sexuality* (May 1983), p. 155.
9. Ephesians 3:20,21.
10. See Philippians 4:19.
11. Proverbs 12:15.
12. Ephesians 4:15.
13. See Matthew 18:15-17.
14. See Colossians 2:13,14.
15. Matthew 5:23,24.
16. See Romans 8:1.
17. James 5:12.
18. Jeremiah 31:3.
19. 2 Corinthians 12:8-10.
20. Psalm 34:10.
21. 1 Peter 1:3-5.
22. Philippians 1:6.

## CHAPTER 9—MELTING THE WALL OF ICE

1. Luke 6:27.
2. Luke 6:28.

# Great Books For Further Reading...

## SingleLife Today™
### *The Largest Catalog of Christian Books & Tapes for Singles!*

Our desire is that the principles in ***Building A Relationship That Lasts*** have helped you personally. Things of great value take time and require special attention. To assist you further, we would love to send you our Single Life Today Catalog. It gives you information and savings on books and tapes of many other authors covering...

- Quality Relationships
- Personal Development
- Divorce Recovery
- Marriage Preparation
- Finances
- Humor
- Spiritual Development
- Bible Studies

To receive your free copy, simply call toll-free:

# 1-888-758-6329

 Single Life Resources™
*A Division of Campus Crusade For Christ*
Post Office Box 1166, Cary, North Carolina 27512
*"Helping Singles Live Dynamic Lives!"*

✓ Check us out on the web: www.slr.org

# Bring A Single Life Resources
# Conference To Your City

- **Bring New Single Adults into Your Ministry**
- **Motivate Single Adults to Godliness**
- **Strengthen the Commitment of Your Leaders**
- **Increase Church and Community Awareness of Your Ministry**

**Becoming A Friend & Lover Conference**
A Conference to Strengthen Your Relationships

**Understanding The Opposite Sex Conference**
Learning To Love A Woman..
Learning To Love A Man

**Standing Strong In Today's Culture Conference**

## Single Life Resources™
*A Division of Campus Crusade For Christ*
Post Office Box 1166, Cary, NC 27512

# 919-363-8000

✓ **Check us out: www.slr.org**

**Give us a call for information about our single adult conferences.**

OR - - - - - - - - →

*"Helping Singles Live Dynamic Lives!"*